Excel Quick

Gaylord N. Smith, MBA, CPA
Professor

Albion College — Albion, Michigan

THOMSON

SOUTH-WESTERN

Australia · Canada · Mexico · Singapore · Spain · United Kingdom · United States

THOMSON

SOUTH-WESTERN

Excel Quick, 2e

Gaylord N. Smith

Vice President/Editorial Director:
Jack W. Calhoun

Vice President/Editor-in-Chief:
George Werthman

Acquisitions Editor:
Julie Lindsay

Acting Developmental Editor:
Janice M. Hughes

Marketing Manager:
Mignon Tucker

Production Editor:
Lora Arduser

Manufacturing Coordinator:
Doug Wilke

Compositor:
Cover to Cover Publishing, Inc.

Printer:
Westgroup
Eagan, MN

Design Project Manager:
Stacy Jenkins Shirley

Cover Designer:
Craig Ramsdell/
Ramsdell Design

Cover Photo:
Courtesy of ©PhotoDisc

LCCN: 2003101365

ISBN: 0-324-27032-1

For more information
contact South-Western,
5191 Natorp Boulevard,
Mason, Ohio 45040.
Or you can visit our Internet site at:
http://www.swlearning.com

Contents

Introduction

Excel Quick is designed for busy people. People who need to get something done today—this morning. People who do not want to read 100 pages before learning how to enter some data and print out a simple spreadsheet model.

Most tutorials take days to complete. The goal of Excel Quick is to get users productively up and running within **one hour** (Lesson 1). Completing all the lessons will take the rest of the morning. You should find the lessons tightly sequenced and thorough. Grueling details have been kept to a minimum.

This book uses a TEACH BY EXAMPLE approach. As little time as possible is spent **discussing**; as much time as possible is spent **doing**.

Will you learn all there is to know about Excel using this book? Absolutely not. But it is a safe bet that **most of what you will ever need to know about Excel** is contained in this book. After completing all of the lessons in this manual, you will be able to design some relatively complex spreadsheet models. When you reach the point where you need to learn about some advanced command or feature in detail, go to a more comprehensive user's guide. In the meantime, Excel Quick will serve you well!

This book covers three versions of Excel: **Excel 97**, **Excel 2000**, and **Excel 2002XP**. Although each version of Excel has added new features, the basics are the same. Where differences exist, they will be thoroughly discussed.

LEARN BY DOING

Lesson 1 provides the minimum that you will need to know to use Excel productively. This lesson takes longer to complete than any other lesson (about an hour), but it may be all you will ever need. It covers starting and ending Excel; entering text, numbers, and formulas on a worksheet; correcting errors; using important toolbar buttons; saving your work for later retrieval; and printing worksheet files. It also introduces "what-if" analysis.

Lesson 2 introduces you to the mathematical capabilities of Excel. Lesson 3 shows you how to quickly expand, modify, and enhance worksheets. These lessons should be completed before attempting the remaining lessons.

Lessons 4 and 5 may be completed in any order. Lesson 4 provides extra information on several specific areas of worksheet design, including using art work. Lesson 5 covers how to create, modify, and use charts and graphs.

LEARN BY READING

There are three helpful appendices in this book to assist you. You should find Appendix C particularly interesting. This appendix provides instructions for creating a rich variety of simple, yet useful, Excel applications. The models are easy to understand and recreate. Studying these examples can be a rewarding and productive way to expand your spreadsheet capabilities.

ACKNOWLEDGMENTS

Sincerest thanks go to my editorial team at South-Western. Although the composition of the team has changed over the years, new members always step in with the same level of enthusiasm and support as their predecessors. The continuous professionalism and dedication to the success of this series is both an inspiration and a comfort to me. Thanks guys!

FINAL COMMENT

Enough said. Let's get started!

Lesson 1
BASIC USER SKILLS

LEARNING OBJECTIVES

In this lesson, you will learn to:

- Start the Microsoft® Excel program
- Move the active cell around the worksheet
- Enter text and numbers
- Modify and delete entries
- Change column widths
- Use toolbar buttons to italicize, bold, align, and underline data; to undo errors; to place borders in cells; and to total the values in a column
- Save worksheets for later recall
- Perform what-if analysis
- Print files
- Exit the Microsoft® Excel program

COMPUTER SPREADSHEETS

Imagine a large sheet of accounting paper with many columns and rows. In the business world, this is often referred to as a worksheet or spreadsheet. Paper spreadsheets are commonly used to gather large amounts of financial data and to accumulate the results using a pencil and a calculator.

Computer spreadsheets are similar to paper spreadsheets in structure and format. One big difference with computer spreadsheets is that the columns and rows appear on a computer screen rather than on paper. Another difference is that arithmetic calculations (totals, averages, etc.) can be performed automatically by the computer. In fact, the real benefit to using a computer spreadsheet comes when you start taking advantage of the program's ability to automatically perform calculations using different sets of numbers (called what-if analysis) and to create charts (graphs) based on data contained in the worksheet. A computer spreadsheet program such as Microsoft® Excel lends itself perfectly to just about any application that requires the analysis and manipulation of numbers.

Check out Appendix C to see some simple and useful Excel applications.

BEFORE BEGINNING

1. *Necessity of Saving Your Work.* During the lessons in this tutorial, you will be asked occasionally to save your work for use in a later lesson. Files should be saved on your hard drive or network. If access to these is not available, you will need to save your work on a properly formatted diskette.

2. *ESC (Escape) Key.* As you work through this tutorial, you will be asked to enter commands using the mouse or various keys on the keyboard. Occasionally, you may make a mistake by clicking the wrong spot or pressing the wrong key. When this occurs, you can use the ESC (Escape) key to escape from the incorrect entry. Pressing the ESC key once or twice will eliminate the error. This will allow you to start over with the proper entry.

3. *Getting Help.* Excel uses the function key marked F1 as a help key. The same help system is available by clicking the Help command in the Menu Bar at the top of the screen.

STARTING MICROSOFT® EXCEL

This tutorial covers three versions of Excel: Excel 97, Excel 2000, and Excel 2002XP. Although each version of Excel has added new features, the basics are the same. Since the menu options and toolbars are generally the same in all three versions, illustrations will be shown using Excel 97. Where differences exist, they will be thoroughly discussed in the tutorial.

Excel

To start Excel, simply double-click the Microsoft® Excel icon. You will see the Excel opening logo for a few seconds followed by a screen containing a blank worksheet window. If necessary, maximize the worksheet screen so that the work area is as large as possible. Illustration 1.1 identifies some important elements of the screen that are unique to Excel. Please take a minute to note the names of the various parts of the Excel screen. Many of these names will be referred to later in the tutorial. Each version of Excel will look slightly different.

Before beginning this tutorial, you should write in the space provided below which version of Microsoft® Excel you are using (Excel 97, Excel 2000, and Excel 2002XP). To find out which version you are using, click **About Microsoft Excel** (**Help** menu).

I am using Version

For Excel 2000 and Excel 2002XP, if you have an annoying little paperclip character on your screen, you can remove it by selecting **Hide the Office Assistant** (**Help** menu). For Excel 2002XP, the default screen may show a Startup Task Pane on the right side of the screen under the heading New Workbook. Close it for now by clicking the "X" to the right of the words New Workbook. (To eliminate the Startup Task Pane on a more permanent basis, click on Options (Tool menu)

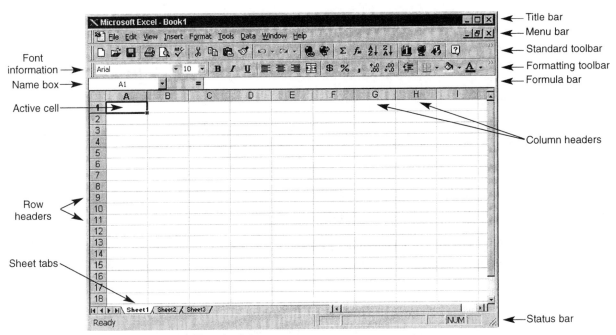

Illustration 1.1   *Worksheet Terminology*

and select View. Under the Show category, uncheck the Startup Task Pane and click OK.)

THE WORKSHEET

Excel uses a grid of columns and rows to frame a work area that is known as the worksheet. Each worksheet is displayed in its own worksheet window. The top border of the worksheet window contains a row of sequential letters (A, B, C, etc.). These are the column headers. The left border of the worksheet window contains a column of sequential numbers (1, 2, 3, etc.). These are the row headers. The intersection of a column and row is known as a cell. Currently the worksheet is completely empty except for an outlined rectangular box in cell A1. This box is known as the active cell. The active cell indicates where text or numbers may be entered on the worksheet. You will also notice that the position of this cell is indicated in the Name box just above the worksheet.

DIFFERENTIATING BETWEEN WORKBOOKS AND WORKSHEETS

Excel files are called workbooks. Each workbook can contain several pages which are referred to as worksheets. Currently on your screen is a workbook named Book1, and it contains several empty worksheets. Notice the workbook name in the Title bar at the top of the screen and the Sheet tabs at the bottom of the worksheet. Both workbooks and worksheets can be given more descriptive names, but for now the default names will be used.

MOVING AROUND THE WORKSHEET

There are several ways to move around the worksheet using either the mouse or the keyboard. Both approaches are demonstrated below.

Using the Mouse

You can use the mouse to move the active cell around the worksheet simply by aiming the mouse pointer at the cell you want to move to and then clicking the left mouse button. To demonstrate this, click **cell B1** (if you miss, aim and try again). After doing this, the active cell should shift to a position under the B column (notice the cell address in the Name box changes from A1 to B1). You can use this method to move the active cell to any location on the worksheet.

The actual worksheet is bigger than what is shown on the screen. To demonstrate this, click the **right scroll arrow** once and notice that column A is no longer visible and that a new column has been added on the right side of the worksheet.

Right scroll arrow

Now for one of the surprises of this program. Repeatedly click the **right scroll arrow** and note that new columns appear in alphabetic sequence (you can speed up the scrolling by holding down the mouse button). Stop when you get to column BD. You have moved out 56 columns. The far right column is IV. That's 256 columns!

The worksheet also has more rows than are shown on the screen. Repeatedly click the **down scroll arrow** to move down the worksheet. Notice the row numbers increase each time you click the down scroll arrow (again, hold down the mouse button to speed up the scrolling). Stop when you get to row 100. It would take a long time for you to find the bottom of the worksheet since it is 65,536 rows deep.

Down scroll arrow

As you can see, the worksheet is very large. There are millions of cells available for use on each worksheet. It is limited only by the memory of your computer. What you see on the screen in the worksheet window is only a small portion of the entire workbook.

As with other Windows programs, you can use the scroll bar to move quickly around the worksheet. Dragging the scroll boxes horizontally or vertically over the scroll bars or clicking the scroll arrows are some common ways of moving around. Feel free to experiment with these now. Position the active cell back in cell A1 when you are done.

Using the Keyboard

You can also use the arrow keys on the keyboard to move the active cell around the worksheet. The arrow keys are located on the right side of your keyboard.

Pressing any of the arrow keys will move the active cell in the direction of the arrow. This is different than clicking the scroll arrows with the mouse. When you click the scroll arrows with the mouse, the active cell remains stationary and the worksheet moves. When you use the arrow keys on the keyboard, the active cell itself moves.

To demonstrate using arrow keys, press the **right arrow** (→) key once. This shifts the active cell over to column B. Now press the **right arrow** (→) key repeatedly and notice that as new columns come on the screen, the active cell remains visible.

There are also four common ways to move the active cell quickly around the worksheet using the keyboard. These methods are particularly helpful for moving the active cell long distances.

1.   The first way is to simply hold down one of the arrow keys on the keyboard. Holding down an arrow key moves the active cell quickly in the direction of the arrow. Try it with the **down arrow** (↓) key.

2.   A second way is to use the keys marked **PG UP** (Page Up) and **PG DN** (Page Down) on the keyboard. These move the active cell up and down one page at a time, respectively. Try these keys out if you wish.

3.   The third way to move long distances quickly is to use the END key in conjunction with the arrow keys. No matter where the active cell is now, press the **END** key once and then press the **down arrow** (↓) key. What happens? As you can see, the END key/arrow key combination moves the active cell to the end of the column or row that the active cell is on. The active cell will stop if it bumps into a cell that isn't empty. Practice using the END key. See if you can get the active cell positioned in the lower right corner of the worksheet.

4.   The fourth way is to hold down the CTRL key and then press the HOME key. Try this **CTRL+HOME** key combination now and watch what happens. This moves the active cell back to cell A1. This is a rather limited, but very helpful, key combination.

      If this does not work for you, try the HOME key by itself.

DATA ENTRY

You are now ready to learn how to enter data on the worksheet. All data entered on a worksheet is classified as either text or values. You must be in the Ready mode to enter data on the worksheet. Check the mode indicator on the left-hand corner of the Status bar. If it does not say Ready, press the ESC key (repeatedly if necessary).

Text

Text is cell input that is either letters or words. In some cases, numbers can be entered as text. Excel does different things with values (i.e., mathematical operations, special number formats, etc.) than with text so it is important that it knows which cells contain text and which are values. By default, text is aligned to the left side of a cell. As you will see later, the alignment of text can be changed so that it is right-aligned or centered.

Values

Values are cell inputs that are either numbers, user-created formulas, or built-in formulas (called functions). By default, values are aligned to the right side of a cell, but this too can be changed.

ENTERING TEXT ON THE WORKSHEET

There are many conventions that relate to entering text and numbers that you need to be aware of. Since the easiest way to introduce you to these is with a demonstration, let's begin entering some data on the worksheet. You will create a simple financial plan for a consulting firm for the first quarter of the year.

To begin with, you will enter the label Consulting fees in cell A2. To do this, move the active cell to cell A2 (use arrow keys or the mouse) and type the letter C. If you make any typing errors, press the **ESC** key and start over. As soon as you type the letter C, the word Enter appears in the mode indicator on the Status bar.

	A	B	C	D	E	F	G
1							
2	C						

Now finish entering your label by typing the letters **onsulting fees**. You will see the words "Consulting fees" appear in the cells and in the Formula bar.

	A	B	C	D	E	F	G
1							
2	Consulting fees						

Storing Input in a Cell

Input is not actually stored in the cell until you (1) press the ENTER key, or (2) press one of the arrow keys, or (3) click the Enter box in the Formula bar, or (4) click some other cell. Pressing ENTER will store the input in the cell and move the active cell down one row. Pressing one of the arrow keys serves the dual purpose of storing input in a cell and moving the active cell in the direction of the arrow. This is particularly helpful when entering a large amount of data in a row or column. Clicking the Enter box stores the input in the active cell without moving it. Clicking the Cancel box serves the same purpose as pressing the ESC key. Use any of these four methods now to store the label Consulting fees in cell A2.

Enter

Cancel

Throughout the rest of this tutorial all instructions for entering input onto the work-sheet will be condensed. You will simply be instructed to enter input into a cell. How you choose to store the entry will be left up to you (using any of the four methods just described).

Continue setting up the financial plan categories by entering **Expenses** in cell A4, **Salaries** in cell A5, **Commissions** in cell A6, **Social security taxes** in cell A7, **Rent** in cell A8, **Total expenses** in cell A9, and **Net income** in cell A11. If you make any typing errors, press ENTER and leave them for now. You will be shown how to correct them later.

	A	B	C	D	E	F	G
1							
2	Consulting fees						
3							
4	Expenses						
5	Salaries						
6	Commissions						
7	Social security taxes						
8	Rent						
9	Total expenses						
10							
11	Net income						

Entering Long Labels

Notice that several labels extend over into column B. The extra characters aren't actually entered in column B, they are just displayed there. Now move the active cell to cell B9 and enter the word **micro**. From the result, you can see that long entries in a cell will not be completely displayed if the adjacent cell contains input.

9	Total expe	micro

Correcting Typing Errors Before Storing

If you make a typing error *before* you press ENTER you can use either the ESC key or the BACKSPACE key to change your entry. Pressing the ESC key will completely cancel the current entry and return you to the Ready mode so you can start over. Pressing the BACKSPACE key will delete the current entry one character at a time (working right to left), allowing you to correct your entry without having to start over from scratch.

Correcting Typing Errors After Storing

There are many ways to correct errors that you catch *after* you store the input in the cell. Two easy methods will be described here. The first method is to simply type over the incorrect entry with a new entry. To demonstrate this, you will change the label in cell A7 from Social security taxes to Payroll taxes. To do this, simply move to cell A7 and enter **Payroll taxes**.

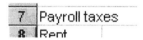

The second way to correct errors is to directly edit the contents of a cell. Move the active cell to cell B9. Let's change the word micro to macro. To activate the Edit mode, press the **F2** key—or double-click the cell—or move the mouse over the word micro in the Formula bar and click once. The mode indicator changes from Ready to Edit. Next, use the **left arrow** (←) key or the mouse to move the *insertion bar* to the space between the letters i and c. The position of the insertion bar is important because pressing the DELETE key erases letters to the right and pressing the BACKSPACE key erases letters to the left. Since you want to change micro to macro, press **BACKSPACE** now to erase the letter i, type the letter a, and press **ENTER**.

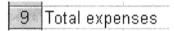

Erasing Cell Contents Completely

Sometimes correcting errors can mean erasing cell contents completely. The DELETE key can be used for this. Move to cell B9 and press the **DELETE** key. Goodbye macro!

TYPEFACE STYLES (FONTS)

The name of the font currently being used by the worksheet is Arial and the size of the type is 10 points. These are shown in the font style and font size boxes. If either of these boxes is not shown on the toolbar, they can be found by clicking the More Buttons or Toolbar Options button.

To demonstrate how to change fonts within individual cells, move to cell A2. Then click the **Font style** drop-down box. Up pops a menu of other font choices. Click one that interests you. The label Consulting fees is immediately presented in the new font. The type size can also be changed by clicking the **Font size** drop-down box and selecting another size. The row height will automatically change to accommodate larger type sizes. Go ahead and experiment.

When you are done experimenting, set cells A2, A4, and A11 to the **Arial** font with a point size of **12**. Your screen should look *exactly* as shown below before proceeding!

More options

Font style box

Font size box

Font size box

	A	B	C	D	E	F	G
1							
2	Consulting fees						
3							
4	Expenses						
5	Salaries						
6	Commissions						
7	Payroll taxes						
8	Rent						
9	Total expenses						
10							
11	Net income						

CHANGING COLUMN WIDTH AND ROW HEIGHT

The titles Expenses, Commissions, Payroll taxes, and Total expenses all spill over into column B. Column widths can be changed to accommodate long words or numbers. Let's widen column A so that the expense titles are completely contained within it. To do this, *move* the mouse pointer to the line between column headers for columns A and B at the top of the worksheet. When positioned exactly on the line, the mouse pointer becomes a thick cross with arrowheads at both ends of the horizontal bar. When this symbol appears, press the mouse button to *grab* the right border of column A, drag the column border to the right about an inch, and then release the mouse button. Column A is now widened and the expense titles no longer overlap into column B.

Another way column widths can be changed is by selecting Column (Format menu) and clicking on Width. The standard column width is 8.43 when the font is Arial size 10.

There is also a way to size columns automatically. Move the mouse pointer again to the line at the top of the worksheet between column headers A and B. When the mouse pointer becomes a thick cross with arrowheads again, double-click the mouse. This technique automatically makes column A just wide enough to include the widest label in that column. See the illustration on the next page.

These same techniques can be used to change the height of any row.

	A	B	C	D	E	F	G
1							
2	Consulting fees						
3							
4	Expenses						
5	Salaries						
6	Commissions						
7	Payroll taxes						
8	Rent						
9	Total expenses						
10							
11	Net income						

ENTERING NUMBERS ON THE WORKSHEET

Now let's give a little substance to your financial plan by adding some numbers.

Entering Numbers

Whenever you need to enter a number on a worksheet, simply enter it using either the numerical keypad on the far right side of your keyboard (NUM LOCK on) or the number keys across the top of your keyboard.

You do not need to include commas or dollar signs as you type in the value, but Excel will accept them. Also, if you enter a decimal point, that will be shown as well. You can enter negative numbers either by enclosing them in parentheses or by preceding the number with a minus sign. You can enter percentages either by typing in the number followed by a % (percent sign) or simply by typing in the percentage as a decimal.

Number Formats

Number formats are the presentation styles for values entered into cells. For example, the value 1234 is shown below expressed in several common format categories.

Value	Category
1234	General
1,234	Number
$1,234	Currency
$ 1,234	Accounting
123400%	Percentage

All of these formats can be shown with decimals, too (e.g., 1234.567 or $1,234.56). Notice also that some of the values are not aligned exactly below each other. Methods to correct this alignment problem are discussed in Lesson 2.

You can designate the number format for cells using the Format command on the main menu. In some cases you can also assign number formats to cells automatically by the way you enter values for the first time. To demonstrate this, enter the following values in the indicated cells (be sure to use dollar signs and commas where shown):

cell C2: **$10,000**	(use dollar sign and comma)
cell C5: **$4,400**	(use dollar sign and comma)
cell C6: **600**	(no dollar sign or comma)
cell C7: **500**	(no dollar sign or comma)
cell C8: **1,350**	(use comma)

	A	B	C	D	E	F	G
1			1st Qtr				
2	Consulting fees		$10,000				
3							
4	Expenses						
5	Salaries		$4,400				
6	Commissions		600				
7	Payroll taxes		500				
8	Rent		1,350				
9	Total expenses						
10							
11	Net income						

Now experiment in cell C8 by entering **1350**, **$1,350**, and **$1,350.00**. Once a number style is established for a cell, all subsequent entries in that cell will show up in the established format until you formally change it. Changing formats will be demonstrated in Lesson 2.

Entering Numbers as Text

Numbers are usually entered as values, but they can also be mixed with letters and entered as text. Common reasons for doing this might be to enter inventory part numbers, addresses, or calendar dates. When numbers and letters are mixed in an entry, Excel is generally smart enough to recognize that entry as text. For example, enter **1st Qtr** in cell C1.

If you wish to treat an entry that contains only numbers as text, you can precede the number with an apostrophe ('). The apostrophe itself does not show up in the cell.

SAVE YOUR WORK

You should get in the habit of saving your work at regular intervals to prevent losing it due to a power failure and other unforeseen mishaps. Select **Save As** (**File** menu). If you can access your hard drive or network, select the **drive** and **directory** where you want to save it. If you wish to save your file on a diskette, insert it into drive A or B and select the appropriate drive. In the File Name text box, type the name **Plan1** and select **Save**.

USING TOOLBAR BUTTONS

Toolbar buttons are shortcuts that can be used to perform many main menu commands quickly. Toolbar buttons are normally placed at the top of the worksheet, but they can be moved, hidden, and customized in many ways.

To find out what each toolbar button does, place the mouse pointer on the button. A short description of the function of that button appears in a small box below the mouse pointer. Take a moment right now and check the function of each button. Do not click any toolbar button with the mouse yet. The Help system in Excel is another valuable source of information on all the toolbar buttons.

Now let's use some of the toolbar buttons to enhance our preliminary financial plan. Again, if these are not on your toolbar, you will find them by clicking More Buttons or Toolbar Options button.

1. Move to cell C1, then click the **Bold** button. Instantly the title 1st Qtr is changed to bold print.

Bold

2. In cell C1 again, click the **Center** button. Now the title 1st Qtr is centered in the cell.

Center

3. In cell C1 again, click the **Borders** button drop-down arrow. Select the single, thin bottom border (second from left, top row). A line is now drawn across the bottom of cell C1.

Borders

4. Move to cell C8, then click the **Underline** button. The number 1,350 is now underlined. Notice that Underline is different than Borders. Underline places a line directly under the characters within a cell. Borders underlines the entire cell.

Underline

5. Ugh! That underline doesn't look great. If total expenses turns out to be a large number, the underline will look really short. Click the **Undo** button. You can also turn off the underline by clicking the **Underline** button again.

Undo

6. In cell C8, click the **Borders** button drop-down arrow. Select the same thin bottom border you did in step 3 above. Repeat this as well in cell C9.

Borders

7. Move to cell C11 and again click the **Borders** drop-down arrow. This time select the double, thin bottom border (far left, middle row). A double line is now drawn across the bottom of cell C11.

Borders

8. Let's italicize the expense titles (range A5 to A8). Two methods will be used to demonstrate selecting this range. First, move to cell A5. Then, hold down the **SHIFT** key, press the **down arrow** (↓) key three times to expand the range to cell A8. The range A5 to A8 is now selected, and cells A6, A7, and A8 should be darkened. (The first cell in a range is always outlined while all other cells in the range are darkened.) If you were to click the Italic button now (don't do it), all four expense titles would be changed to italic. Deselect the range now by clicking anywhere on the worksheet.

4	Expenses
5	Salaries
6	Commissions
7	Payroll taxes
8	Rent
9	Total expenses

Now let's use the mouse to select the same range. Aim the mouse pointer at cell A5, depress the mouse button, drag the mouse pointer down to cell A8, and then release the mouse button. If you have any problems, try again. After the range has been properly selected, click the **Italic** button. The four expense titles are now changed to italic print.

Italic

9. Move to cell A9, then click the **Align Right** button. This moves the label Total expenses to the right side of cell A9.

Align Right

FUNCTIONS AND FORMULAS

Two values are needed to finish the financial plan: Total expenses and Net income.

Functions

Move to cell C9, then click the **AutoSum** button and press **ENTER**. Instantly the column of numbers is totalled using a function called SUM (more on this and other functions in Lesson 2). Since the top number in this column is in the Currency format, Excel places the sum in the same format.

AutoSum

Formulas

Now you are ready to write a formula containing cell references that will be used to compute net income. Please note that the formula must be preceded with an = (equal) sign. Formulas will be covered in more detail in Lesson 2.

Since net income is revenue minus total expenses, the formula you are going to write will tell Excel to take the value in cell C2 (revenue), subtract the value in cell C9 (total expenses), and put the result in cell C11. This is easy to do. Move to cell C11, type the formula **=C2-C9** (you may use either capital or lowercase letters when entering formulas), and press **ENTER**. Excel will instantly perform the calculation and the result ($3,150) should appear in cell C11. Note that the formula =C2-C9 appears in the Formula bar.

If you had forgotten to type the = (equal) sign when entering the formula, Excel would think that you were entering text and C2-C9 would appear in cell C11 instead of the value $3,150.

Your financial plan should appear as below.

	A	B	C	D	E	F	G
1			**1st Qtr**				
2	Consulting fees		$10,000				
3							
4	Expenses						
5	*Salaries*		$4,400				
6	*Commissions*		600				
7	*Payroll taxes*		500				
8	*Rent*		1,350				
9	Total expenses		$6,850				
10							
11	Net income		$3,150				

Note that dollar signs ($) are used only at the top and the bottom, and for items being subtotaled. This is the standard professional format for financial statements.

SAVE YOUR WORKBOOK AGAIN

Since you have made some changes to your file since you last saved it, your new version should be saved. On the toolbar, click the **Save** button (or on the File menu, click Save).

Save

PRINTING A WORKSHEET

You are now finished with your first spreadsheet model. It looks pretty nice! Let's get a printout of it. Click the **Print** button on the Toolbar and examine your printed masterpiece.

Print

A printed spreadsheet page will contain nine normal-sized columns and will extend down about 50 rows before going to a second page (if those rows contain any data). Because printing a spreadsheet file is not the same as printing a word processing document, there are some print options and controls of which you should be aware.

To briefly go over these, select **Page Setup** (**File** menu), and click the **Page** tab. Two important settings will be discussed here; you can try them later when you work with a larger model than the one you currently have. First, spreadsheet models are frequently wider than they are tall, so selecting **Landscape** orientation (i.e., printing sideways on a page) can be very helpful. Second, it is not uncommon to have spreadsheet models extend beyond one page when printing, and yet, if downsized for printing purposes only, they could fit nicely on one page with smaller print. Clicking the **Fit To 1 Page** option works great for this purpose.

Click the **Margin** tab. Here you set your margins as you wish.

Click the **Header/Footer** tab. Headers and footers are print items that appear at the top and bottom of every printed page. Most people want none. To set your header to None (if it is not already set that way), click the **Header** drop-down arrow and use the scroll bar to find (none) at the top of the options list. Click on it. Use the same process for setting your footer. Do this now for your model if you wish.

Click the **Sheet** tab. The first important option on this tab is *Gridlines*. Selecting this will print the column and row lines when the worksheet is printed. This is particularly helpful on a wide worksheet. A second helpful option is *Row and Column Headings*. Selecting this will print the column letters and row numbers when the worksheet is printed. Your model does not need the gridline or row and column heading options, but you are welcome to experiment later. For now, click **OK** to close the Page Setup dialog box.

Before demonstrating some additional print options, click in **cell N1** and enter your **name**. It is always a good idea to preview a document before you print it. On the Standard toolbar, click the **Print Preview** button. A Preview window appears and you can see what your worksheet looks like before you print it. On the screen you see your financial planning model. Click the **Next** button and you will see page 2 of the printout which contains your name. Now, select the **Page Break Preview** option. The blue borders (solid or dashed) indicate what will be printed on each page. For future reference, these blue borders are page breaks and can be moved with a mouse to print exactly what you want on each page. For now, select **View** and then **Normal** to get back to the regular worksheet. Other commands you should be aware of are Insert Page Break and Insert Remove Page Break. Page break changes are saved when your file is saved.

Print Preview

You can also print just a portion of the worksheet if you wish. For example, let's assume you want to print only the expenses shown in your model. On your worksheet, select the range **A4 to C9** and then click **Print** (**File** menu). Under the **Print What** area of the Print dialog box, click **Selection** and then click **OK**.

WHAT-IF ANALYSIS

One of the most important features of spreadsheet programs is their ability to quickly recalculate values when new data are entered. This is often referred to as what-if analysis—"What if the value were this? What if the value were that?" Although our financial plan model is still very simple, this recalculation ability can be easily demonstrated. Suppose rent expense is $1,500 instead of $1,350. Enter **1500** in cell C8 now. Instantly, total expenses are changed to $7,000 and net income changes to $3,000! Enter **11000** in cell C2 (Consulting fees) now. Bingo! Net income changes to $4,000. Experiment with other values if you wish. You will find that the total expenses and net income are recomputed each time. Think of the possibilities!

FINISHING THE LESSON

To continue on directly to Lesson 2, select **Close** (**File** menu). If you are going to do Lesson 2 at a later time, select **Exit** (**File** menu). If you are asked if you want to "Save changes," choose **No** since you do *not* want your "what-if" numbers saved. You want to keep the original financial plan numbers intact.

FINAL COMMENT

Give yourself a pat on the back. This first lesson has covered a lot of territory. You should feel confident enough at this point in time to construct some simple but useful spreadsheet models. You will find the remaining lessons in this tutorial are shorter, but no less important.

If you have a disk of Excel files created by other people which you wish to use, you are prepared to do this now. However, if you wish to expand your spreadsheeting skills so that you can design models like those seen in Appendix C, read on!

Lesson 2
MATH: FORMULAS, FORMATS, AND FUNCTIONS

LEARNING OBJECTIVES

In this lesson, you will learn to:

- Use Excel to perform arithmetic calculations
- Design Excel formulas
- Distinguish between number formats
- Use Excel functions
- Display formulas and cell contents

BEFORE BEGINNING

In this lesson you are going to expand the financial plan that you created in Lesson 1 and saved as a workbook named Plan1. You should have that file available on your file diskette, hard drive, or network. To begin this lesson, the Excel program should be started and a blank worksheet should be on your screen (use the File New command if necessary, and then click OK on the General tab. Do not open the Plan1 workbook yet.

THE IMPORTANCE OF FORMULAS IN EXCEL

The ability to enter formulas on worksheets is one of the most important features of Excel. It is what makes spreadsheet programs so flexible and powerful, and so appropriate for performing repeated numerical analysis, sometimes called what-if analysis. This form of analysis was introduced in Lesson 1.

When you enter a formula in a cell, Excel automatically computes the answer and immediately displays it in the cell. The formula itself will be displayed in the Formula bar. The worksheet models shown in Appendix C use many formulas.

Writing formulas in Excel is usually very easy, but you can make your formulas as complicated as your needs demand. Formulas can include any combination of the following: numbers, mathematical operators, cell references, functions, and range names. All of these except range names will be covered in this lesson. Range names will be covered in Lesson 4.

MATH

The simplest type of formula that you can create in Excel is one that only contains numbers and mathematical operators. The basic mathematical operations that Excel can perform are addition, subtraction, multiplication, division, and exponentiation. Table 2.1 indicates the keyboard keys for each mathematical operation. You will find all of the operator keys on the keyboard, some in more than one place.

Try each of the examples listed in Table 2.1 by entering them on the blank worksheet on your monitor. Be sure to include the = sign at the beginning of each entry. After you press ENTER for each example, notice that the keys you typed appear in the Formula bar and that the answer appears in the cell you used for entry.

Table 2.1   Mathematical Operations

Symbol		Description	Example	Explanation	Answer
+	Plus Sign	Addition	=123+456	Adds 123 and 456	579
-	Minus Sign	Subtraction	=123-81	Subtracts 81 from 123	42
*	Asterisk	Multiplication	=123*1.2	Multiplies 123 by 1.2	147.6
/	Slash	Division	=123/7	Divides 123 by 7	17.57143
^	Caret	Exponentiation	=123^2	Squares 123	15129

Order of Precedence

All of the examples in Table 2.1 use only one mathematical operator at a time to perform a single operation. You can also combine the operator keys to perform several mathematical operations at once. For example, enter **=4+6/2-1** in cell A1 (result is 6).

If you are going to use more than one operator in a formula, you should be aware of the sequence that Excel will use to perform computations. This is called the order of precedence, and for Excel, it is as follows:

First: Exponentiation
Second: Multiplication and Division
Third: Addition and Subtraction

Just like high school algebra! Within each level of precedence, the calculations are performed from left to right. In the formula =4+6/2-1, the first operation performed is 6 divided by 2 (result is 3). Next, starting from the left, 4 is added to 3 (result is 7), and then 1 is subtracted from 7 (result is 6).

Use of Parentheses

If you wish to perform the computations in some other sequence, what can you do? Rearranging the mathematical operators is not always the answer. However, you can control the sequence of computations by using parentheses. There are several things that you need to know about the use of parentheses in Excel. These are listed below. Try each example on your worksheet.

1. Excel will always perform calculations inside a set of parentheses before doing any other arithmetic operations. Suppose in the example above that you want to add 4 and 6 before dividing by 2. Using parentheses, the formula would look as follows: =(4+6)/2-1 (result is 4).

2. It is also possible to have several sets of parentheses in a single formula, such as = 2*(9+7)/(4-2). Excel will perform the operations inside both pairs of parentheses first (left set first), then do the multiplication, and lastly do the division (result is 16).

3. Parentheses may also be nested as shown in this example: =90/((9+6)*3). Excel will perform the operations in the innermost set of parentheses first and will then work outward to the next set. In this example, the program will add 9 and 6, multiply the result by 3, and then divide that answer into 90 (result is 2).

4. There must always be an equal number of left and right parentheses in a formula. The formula =(128/4*(3+81) is incorrect because there are two left parentheses and only a single right parenthesis. When you enter this formula, Excel will respond with an error message. Click **No**, then **OK**, and then press **ESC**.

FORMULAS

Open Plan1

Now let's expand and improve the simple financial plan you created in Lesson 1. To do this you must close the current workbook that you have been entering formulas into and open the Plan1 workbook. Follow the steps listed below:

1. Select **Close** (**File** menu) and select **No** when asked "Save changes in Book1?"

2. Select **Open** (**File** menu) and select **Plan1** from the drive where you saved it in Lesson 1. It should appear as shown in Illustration 2.1.

Expanding the Financial Planning Model

In Lesson 1, you played what-if with your model by entering in different values for consulting fees and for the various expenses. You probably noted that when you changed only consulting fees it changed net income, but it did not change total expenses. This is because none of the expenses are currently linked in any way to the value of consulting fees.

	A	B	C	D	E	F	G
1			**1st Qtr**				
2	Consulting fees		$10,000				
3							
4	Expenses						
5	Salaries		$4,400				
6	Commissions		600				
7	Payroll taxes		500				
8	Rent		1,350				
9	Total expenses		$6,850				
10							
11	Net income		$3,150				

Illustration 2.1 *Plan1*

Suppose that for our little company, commissions should be based on consulting fees (6% of revenue, hence $600), and payroll taxes should be paid on both salaries and commissions (10% of the combined total, hence $500). As you play what-if with the consulting fees, these expenses should also change. You can enter formulas to do just that.

Formula Pointing

Formulas can be entered from the keyboard as you did in Lesson 1 when you typed in the formula for net income. Excel also provides an alternate way to enter formulas. Instead of typing in the cell addresses like you did in Lesson 1, Excel allows you to simply point to the cells you want to enter. You can use either the mouse or the arrow keys on the keyboard to do the pointing. You will now use both approaches to enter appropriate formulas for commissions and for payroll taxes.

First, you will use the mouse to enter a formula to compute commissions expense. Use the following steps to enter the formula =C2*0.06 in cell C6:

1. Click on cell C6.

2. Type = (equal sign).

3. Click cell C2.

4. Type * (asterisk).

5. Type **.06**.

6. Click the **Confirm** box in the Formula bar or press **ENTER**.

The formula =C2*0.06 shows up in the Formula bar and the answer ($600.00) appears in cell C6.

`=C2*0.06`

Let's use the arrow keys now to enter a formula to automatically compute payroll taxes. Payroll taxes are computed by multiplying the sum of salaries and commissions by 10%. Use the following steps to enter the formula =(C5+C6)*0.1 in cell C7:

1. Move to cell C7.

2. Type = (equal sign).

3. Type ((left parenthesis).

4. Use the arrow keys to move to cell C5.

5. Type + (plus sign).

6. Use the arrow keys to move to cell C6.

7. Type) (right parenthesis).

8. Type * (asterisk).

9. Type **.1** or **10%**.

10. Press **ENTER**.

The formula =(C5+C6)*0.1 shows up in the Formula bar and the answer (500) appears in cell C7.

`=(C5+C6)*0.1`

This pointing technique with the mouse or the arrow keys can be used any time you use a cell address in a command sequence, formula, or function. Most people make extensive use of pointing. However, you should use whichever approach you feel most comfortable with (typing cell addresses in, pointing with the mouse, or pointing with the arrow keys).

NUMBER FORMATS

There are some problems, both visible and hidden, with the number formats in cells C6, C7, and C8. To reveal the hidden problem, enter **$10,001** in cell C2. See Illustration 2.2.

	A	B	C	D	E	F	G
1			1st Qtr				
2	Consulting fees		$10,001				
3							
4	Expenses						
5	Salaries		$4,400				
6	Commissions		$600.06				
7	Payroll taxes		500.006				
8	Rent		1,350				
9	Total expenses		$6,850				
10							
11	Net income		$3,151				

Illustration 2.2   *Plan1 with Inconsistent Alignment, Format, and Decimal Places*

The problems in the model are: cell C6 was switched to the Currency format by Excel when you entered the formula; cell C6 has two decimal places; C7 shows three decimal places. The values in C7 and C8 do not line up directly under the values in C5 and C6.

All of this makes for a very sloppy, unprofessional presentaton. Normal financial statements show dollar signs at the top of columns and at the bottom for subtotals and totals. Numbers in columns should all have the same decimal place. These objectives can be met by using proper number formats. To see all the available number formats, select the **Cells** option (**Format** menu) and click the **Number** tab. Check out some of the categories by clicking on them. After viewing various categories, select **Cancel**. A description of each option is shown in Table 2.2.

Table 2.2   Number Formats

Category	**Description**
General	No specific number format; aligns value to far right side of cell

Examples:	1234
	1234.567

Number	Can specify decimal place, use of commas, and alignment of value to far right side of cell or one space in*

Examples:	1,234
	1,234
	1234.01

Category	Description
Currency	Uses commas; can specify decimal place, use of $ (placed directly in front of number), and alignment of value to far right side of cell or one space in*

Examples:	$1,234
	$1,234
	$1,234.01

Accounting	Uses commas; can specify decimal place and use of $ (placed to far left side of cell). All values are aligned one space in from far right side of cell

Examples:	$	1,234
		1,234
	$	1,234.01

Date	Various date presentation formats
Time	Various time presentation formats
Percentage	Numbers expressed as percentages (e.g., .43 becomes 43%)
Fraction	Decimals expressed as fractions (e.g., .375 becomes 3/8)
Scientific	Displays values in scientific notation (e.g., 5.46E+04)
Text	All entries treated as text
Special	Zip codes, phone numbers, social security numbers, etc.
Custom	Specialized formats

* In the Number and Currency formats, to align values one space in from the right side of the cell, pick an option for which negative values are shown in parentheses.

There are three toolbar buttons that can be used to quickly format values, but the names of two of the buttons can be confusing. If these buttons are not on your toolbar, they can be found by clicking the More Buttons or Toolbar Options button. The Currency Style button places cells in the Accounting (surprise!) format with a $ and two decimal places. The Percent Style button places cells in the Percentage format. The Comma Style button places cells in the Accounting format with no $, but with two decimal places.

Currency Style

Percent Style

Comma Style

Let's use the Comma Style button to uniformly format cells C6 to C8. To accomplish this with your model, use the following steps:

1.   Select the range C6 to C8.

2.   Click the **Comma Style** button.

3.   Click the **Decrease Decimal** button twice.

4.   Click cell C2.

.00
+.0

Decrease Decimal

See Illustration 2.3. Your model is now looking very professional!

	A	B	C	D	E	F	G
1			**1st Qtr**				
2	Consulting fees		$10,001				
3							
4	Expenses						
5	*Salaries*		$4,400				
6	*Commissions*		600				
7	*Payroll taxes*		500				
8	*Rent*		1,350				
9	Total expenses		$6,850				
10							
11	Net income		$3,151				

Illustration 2.3   *Plan1 with Uniform Alignment, Format, and Decimal Places*

SAVE YOUR WORK

Change the **value** in cell C2 to $10,000. Before proceeding, save your new and improved financial plan as Plan2. To do this, select the **Save As** command (**File** menu), choose the proper drive and directory, type the name **Plan2** in the File name text box, and click **Save**. See Illustration 2.4.

	A	B	C	D	E	F	G
1			**1st Qtr**				
2	Consulting fees		$10,000				
3							
4	Expenses						
5	*Salaries*		$4,400				
6	*Commissions*		600				
7	*Payroll taxes*		500				
8	*Rent*		1,350				
9	Total expenses		$6,850				
10							
11	Net income		$3,150				

Illustration 2.4   *Plan2*

Please note that throughout the rest of Lesson 2, you should not save your file again. In the remaining sections of this lesson you will be making some experimental changes to your financial plan that are for demonstration purposes only. These changes are not intended to become a permanent part of the Plan2 file.

PRINT YOUR FILE

This is a good time to print out your model so that you can have a permanent record of your work so far. Review instructions for printing in Lesson 1. On the Standard toolbar, click the **Print** button.

Print

WHAT-IF ANALYSIS AGAIN

Let's do a little more what-if analysis. Move to cell C2 and try the values **11000**, **25000**, and **5000**. Notice now that commissions, payroll taxes, total expenses, and net income all change with the different values entered in cell C2, and the number formats stay consistent.

Numerical Input Quirks

In spite of proper number formats, certain entries in cell C2 will cause strange results. Enter 10,000.52 in cell C2. Notice that the net income answer appears to be off by one dollar. This error is an occasional, annoying occurrence in Excel. It is caused because number formats change the *appearance* of the values in cells, but not the *actual* values. For example, the actual value in cell C2 is 10,000.52, but because of the number format chosen for this cell (Currency with no decimals) Excel rounds off the appearance of the value to the closest whole number. This rounding process is perfectly proper, but it does cause occasional problems, as in this case.

	Actual Value	Appearance
Consulting fees	10,000.52000	$10,001
Salaries	4,400.00000	$4,400
Commissions	600.03120	600
Payroll taxes	500.00312	500
Rent	1,350.00000	1,350
Total expenses	6,850.03432	$6,850
Net income	3,150.48568	$3,150

The appearance of a $1 discrepancy on a financial statement isn't much, but it can cast doubt on other parts of your model to an uninformed reader. If you are interested in correcting this "minor" problem, you may use the ROUND function described in Appendix A.

To demonstrate another input quirk, enter the word **HELLO** in cell C2. The reason that #VALUE! appears in several cells is because Excel does not know how to interpret text in a formula. Many error messages in Excel begin with a #. On the Help menu Index, they are listed first (except in Excel 2002XP).

Enter **=123/0** in cell C2. Dividing a value by zero results in #DIV/0! on your work-sheet. Be aware that this error will ripple through your formulas. Thus, any formula that refers to a cell that contains #DIV/0! will also show #DIV/0!.

Enter **=C11** in cell C2. When entering formulas in Excel, you must make sure not to enter a formula in a cell that refers to itself either directly or indirectly. This is known as a circular reference. In this case the formula in cell C11 uses informa-tion from C2, and now the formula in cell C2 refers to cell C11. Excel warns the user when a circular reference occurs. Click **Cancel**.

Enter **10,000** in cell C2 and **1234567** in cell C5. Two things happen: (1) column C automatically widens to accommodate the long number, and (2) ######## now appears in cell C11. When the value of a formula is too large to show up in a cell, this is how Excel responds. If you widen column C a bit, the value in cell C11 will show up.

Now re-enter **4400** in cell C5. Unfortunately, one of the consequences of entering a large number is that column C is now wider than all the other columns. Reset the column to its original width by selecting the **Column** option (**Format** menu) and then clicking **Width**. Enter **8.43** (assuming your font is Arial size 10) and click **OK**.

USING FUNCTIONS

Besides using the five operator keys (+, -, *, /, and ^), there are more complex mathematical functions that Excel can perform. They are called functions, and they consist of built-in formulas to perform a long list of different tasks automati-cally. A partial list of functions includes SUM (to sum the values in a range of cells), SQRT (to find the square root), AVERAGE (to compute the average value in a range of cells), MAX (to find the maximum value in a range of cells), IF (to enter one value if something is true and another if not), VLOOKUP (to look up val-ues in a table), and NPV (to compute net present value). These and other func-tions are discussed in detail in Appendix A of this manual.

Function Basics

Most functions require you to enter additional information in parentheses that will allow the function to perform its task. Functions can be entered using either cap-ital or lowercase letters. Any cell addresses used in a function may be entered by typing them in or by pointing to them.

Examine the formula entered in cell C9 now. The formula entered in that cell is =SUM(C5:C8). This is the SUM function. C5 is the first cell to be included in the total, and C8 is the last. This function was entered when you used the AutoSum toolbar button back in Lesson 1.

You also could have entered this function by typing in all the characters you now see in cell C9. To demonstrate, move to cell B13, type **=SUM(C5:C8)** and press **ENTER**. The total $6,850 should now appear in the cell.

You also could have entered the formula **=C5+C6+C7+C8**. Try it in cell B14. This method is fine for adding a short series of cells, but using the SUM function is certainly quicker for longer ranges.

You can use the pointing technique to enter all cell references used in functions. To demonstrate the pointing technique using arrow keys, move to cell B15, type **=SUM(** and use the arrow keys to move to cell C5. Type the : (colon) key to lock in the beginning point of the range and press the **down arrow** (↓) key three times to move to cell C8. Finally, type) (right parenthesis) and press **ENTER**.

To demonstrate the pointing technique using the mouse, move the cell pointer to cell B16, type **=SUM(** and select the range to be summed by dragging the mouse pointer over the range C5 to C8. Type) (right parenthesis) and then click the Confirm box.

For the absent-minded, Excel will automatically add the final right parenthesis if you happen to forget to type it in.

Function Help

Help screens are extremely useful as a reference for all the functions that are available in Excel. The Help system is available by selecting Help from the main menu.

A HIDDEN TRICK

There is a quick way to display on the screen all formulas, functions, and other cell contents. Press the **CTRL** key and then press the **Tilde** (~) key—it's right above the Tab key. Bingo! All cell contents are displayed. To return to a normal display, press this key combination again.

FINAL COMMENT

In this lesson, you learned how to construct formulas using numbers, mathematical operators, cell references, and functions. You were also warned about some typical input quirks. Believe it or not, you are now equipped to construct some relatively complicated spreadsheet models. Very few of the models in Appendix C have formulas that are more complicated than what you have seen in this lesson. So get those creative juices flowing!

Since you are not going to save any of the changes that you made in the last two sections of Lesson 2, feel free to experiment with new formulas and functions. When you are done, close this file *without* saving any of the changes that have been made to it. To do this, select the **Exit** or **Close** command (**File** menu) and then select **No** when you are asked to save changes in Plan2.

Lesson 3

EXPANDING AND ENHANCING YOUR MODEL

LEARNING OBJECTIVES

In this lesson, you will learn to:

- Copy data
- Move data
- Insert new columns and rows
- Delete existing columns and rows

BEFORE BEGINNING

In this lesson you are going to take the financial plan that you improved in Lesson 2 and expand it further. To begin this lesson, the Excel program should be started and the workbook Plan2 should be opened on your screen. See Illustration 3.1.

	A	B	C	D	E	F	G
1			**1st Qtr**				
2	Consulting fees		$10,000				
3							
4	Expenses						
5	Salaries		$4,400				
6	Commissions		600				
7	Payroll taxes		500				
8	Rent		1,350				
9	Total expenses		$6,850				
10							
11	Net income		$3,150				
12							

Illustration 3.1   *Plan2*

EXPANDING THE FINANCIAL PLANNING MODEL

Let's expand the financial plan developed in Lesson 2 to include three more quarters and a year total. A single column will be used for each quarter and then a final column for the total. Remember, if you make errors as you make the changes to the model, you can use the Undo toolbar button to undo your last entry. The DELETE key may also come in handy.

You need to enter data for each of the other three quarters. Since you learned about entering text, numbers, and formulas in Lessons 1 and 2, filling in the remaining quarters and computing the year totals would be easy for you. On a worksheet much larger than Plan2, it would be very time-consuming to enter all of this data one cell at a time. Luckily, with computer spreadsheet programs such as Excel, it is very easy to copy data, text, and formulas. This saves time by reducing the need to perform repetitive entry tasks.

COPYING DATA

There are several ways that you can copy data in Excel. Two methods will be demonstrated below and a third method will be discussed:

1. Using the Fill Handle.
2. Using the Copy and Paste buttons or commands.
3. Using the mouse and CTRL key to drag and copy.

Using the Fill Handle

Select cell C1. Position the mouse pointer over the small black box, called a fill handle, in the lower right corner of the cell. The pointer becomes a black cross shape.

Next, drag the fill handle over to cell F1 and then release the mouse button. The headings are automatically filled in for the remaining quarters.

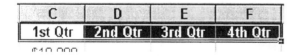

The fill handle has been programmed to recognize numeric and date sequences. In this case, it recognized *1st* and was able to complete the sequence. If the fill handle does not recognize a sequence, you'll just have to type it in yourself! More about the fill handle in Lesson 4.

The fill handle can also be used to copy formulas. To demonstrate this, assume that consulting fees will increase by 5% per quarter. In other words, you want consulting fees to be 5% greater each quarter than in the preceding quarter. To compute 2nd Quarter consulting fees, you want to tell Excel to multiply 1st Quarter consulting fees (cell C2) by 1.05 and place the result in cell D2. To do this, enter **=C2*1.05** now in cell D2.

In Excel 97, the value $10,500 shows in cell C2. This is what we want. In Excel 2000 and Excel 2002XP, the value $10,500.00 shows in cell C2. Correct this now by using the Decrease Decimal button to eliminate the two decimal points. When multiplying by a number with two decimals, Excel will automatically add two decimals to the answer. The same is true for one decimal, three decimals, etc. Isn't Excel wonderful!

Next, this 5% increase should be computed for both of the remaining quarters. These values will be entered using the fill handle. Select cell D2, grab the fill handle in that cell, drag it over to cell F2, and release the mouse button. Instantly cells E2 and F2 display a value for consulting fees that is 5% higher than the value for each previous quarter.

	A	B	C	D	E	F	G
1			1st Qtr	2nd Qtr	3rd Qtr	4th Qtr	
2	Consulting fees		$10,000	$10,500	$11,025	$11,576	

Relative Cell Addresses

Notice the sequence of values for consulting fees. Each quarter is a 5% increase over the previous quarter. The formula in cell D2 is =C2*1.05. Move to cell E2 and check the formula in that cell. You will see that the formula is =D2*1.05. Move to F2 and note that the formula is =E2*1.05.

D	E	F
2nd Qtr	3rd Qtr	4th Qtr
=C2*1.05	=D2*1.05	=E2*1.05

Obviously the formula in cell D2 was not copied exactly. As it moved from cell to cell, the formula was modified to follow the same pattern as in the original formula. In this case, the original formula in cell D2 uses a value from the cell to its immediate left (C2). Therefore, the value in cell E2 will use a value from the cell to its immediate left (D2), and the value in cell F2 will use a value from the cell to its immediate left (E2). When copying formulas unless otherwise specified, Excel assumes that all cell addresses are relative and are to be modified from cell to cell.

Absolute Cell Addresses

But what if you want to copy a formula and leave the cell addresses unaltered? Excel allows you to make cell addresses "absolute" so they will not be modified as they are copied from cell to cell. This is done by adding $ (dollar signs) to any cell address used in a formula. To compare the effects of absolute versus relative copying of formulas, examine Table 3.1.

Table 3.1   Effects of Absolute vs. Relative Cell Addresses

	C2 Is Absolute		C2 Is Relative	
	Formula	Value	Formula	Value
Original Formula	D2: C2*1.05	10500	D2: C2*1.05	10500
Copy	E2: C2*1.05	10500	E2: D2*1.05	11025
Copy	F2: C2*1.05	10500	F2: E2*1.05	11576

Mixed Addresses

On some occasions you may not want the whole cell address to be absolute, just the column part or the row part. This is called a mixed address. In these cases, type a single $ in front of the part of the cell address that you want to be absolute (e.g., $C2 or C$2).

F4 Key (A hidden trick)

There is a quick way to add dollar signs to cell addresses, even those already entered into formulas. When typing in, editing, or pointing to a cell address, pressing the F4 key repeatedly places $ in front of various parts of the cell address automatically.

The Fill Handle Again

You can copy several cells at once. To demonstrate this, let's copy all of the remaining 1st Quarter values and formulas to the other quarters. Select the range C5 to C11, drag the fill handle over to column F, and release the mouse button. See Illustration 3.2.

	A	B	C	D	E	F	G
1			1st Qtr	2nd Qtr	3rd Qtr	4th Qtr	
2	Consulting fees		$10,000	$10,500	$11,025	$11,576	
3							
4	Expenses						
5	Salaries		$4,400	$4,401	$4,402	$4,403	
6	Commissions		600	630	662	695	
7	Payroll taxes		500	503	506	510	
8	Rent		1,350	1,351	1,352	1,353	
9	Total expenses		$6,850	$6,885	$6,922	$6,960	
10							
11	Net income		$3,150	$3,615	$4,103	$4,616	

Illustration 3.2   *Copying with the Fill Handle*

Everything looks okay, but examine rows 5 and 8 closely. Notice that the fill handle increased these expenses $1 each quarter. The fill handle is programmed to increase all numbers by 1 unless it sees some other pattern. This is *not* the result you wanted. A better way to handle this copying is with the normal Copy and Paste commands. Click the **Undo** button to get out of this mess.

Undo

Copy and Paste Buttons and Commands

The Copy and Paste commands are found on the Edit menu. There are also toolbar buttons for each. Since the buttons are easier to use, they'll be used in this section.

Let's begin again the process of copying the first quarter values and formulas to the remaining three quarters.

1. Select the range C5 to C11. Use the mouse or the SHIFT+ARROW key combination to do this.

2. Click the **Copy** toolbar button. This places a copy of the values, formulas, and formats of the selected range into a part of your computer's memory called the clipboard.

Copy

3. Select the range D5 to F5 as the destination. Note that only the top row in a range needs to be selected.

4. Click the **Paste** toolbar button. This command copies whatever is in the clipboard to those cells. Note that borders and formats are copied along with the values and formulas.

Paste

5. Click cell A1 and then examine the formulas in columns D, E, and F. Note how they have been updated as you go from column to column. Illustration 3.3 shows how your screen will appear when you select cells C5 to C11 to copy.

	A	B	C	D	E	F	G
1			1st Qtr	2nd Qtr	3rd Qtr	4th Qtr	
2	Consulting fees		$10,000	$10,500	$11,025	$11,576	
3							
4	Expenses						
5	*Salaries*		$4,400	$4,400	$4,400	$4,400	
6	*Commissions*		600	630	662	695	
7	*Payroll taxes*		500	503	506	509	
8	*Rent*		1,350	1,350	1,350	1,350	
9	Total expenses		$6,850	$6,883	$6,918	$6,954	
10							
11	Net income		$3,150	$3,617	$4,107	$4,622	

Illustration 3.3   *Copy and Paste Quarterly Expenses*

It also should be noted that the dashed outline around the copied range indicates that the clipboard still contains a copy of the contents of those cells. The Edit Paste command can be used over and over again to paste this data elsewhere on the worksheet. The dashed outline will disappear if you press ESC.

If you ever want to copy an entire column or row, click the column header (a letter) or row header (a number) before clicking the Copy button.

It is now time to fill in the Total column. First, move to cell G1 and enter the word **Total**. Then Bold it, Center it, and give it a bottom Border. Then move to cell G2, and review the function section of Lesson 2. Use any method you wish to enter =SUM(C2:F2) in that cell (quickest way: click the AutoSum toolbar button and press ENTER).

B *Bold*   ≡ *Center*

Finally, use any method you wish (the Edit Copy and Paste commands or the toolbar buttons) to copy the formula in cell G2 and paste it to the range G5 to G9 and then paste it again to cell G11. The results are shown in Illustration 3.4.

Borders   *Copy*

Paste

	A	B	C	D	E	F	G
1			1st Qtr	2nd Qtr	3rd Qtr	4th Qtr	Total
2	Consulting fees		$10,000	$10,500	$11,025	$11,576	$43,101
3							
4	Expenses						
5	Salaries		$4,400	$4,400	$4,400	$4,400	$17,600
6	Commissions		600	630	662	695	$2,586
7	Payroll taxes		500	503	506	509	$2,019
8	Rent		1,350	1,350	1,350	1,350	$5,400
9	Total expenses		$6,850	$6,883	$6,918	$6,954	$27,605
10							
11	Net income		$3,150	$3,617	$4,107	$4,622	$15,497

Illustration 3.4   *Filling in the Total Column*

Copying Data with the Mouse and the CTRL key

A third approach to copying data involves using the mouse and the CTRL key. When you position the mouse pointer on the border of a selected cell or range, the mouse pointer becomes an arrow. You then hold down the CTRL key and drag the cell or range to a new location. Wherever you release the mouse button, a copy is made. This feature is very handy, but you are limited because copying can take place only to a single destination. For example, you can copy from cell D2 to cell E2 or to cell F2, but not to both cells at once.

CLEANING UP THE FINANCIAL PLAN

Let's clean up the financial plan so all labels and values are presented in a uniform fashion.

1.   Select the range G6 to G8. Click the **Comma** button and then click the **Decrease Decimals** button twice to get rid of the decimals.

Comma Style   *Decrease Decimals*

2. Move to cell G8, click the **Borders** button, and put a thin, bottom border in the cell. Repeat this with cell G9.

Borders

3. Move to cell G11, click the **Borders** button, and put a thin, double bottom border in the cell.

See Illustration 3.5.

	A	B	C	D	E	F	G
1			1st Qtr	2nd Qtr	3rd Qtr	4th Qtr	Total
2	Consulting fees		$10,000	$10,500	$11,025	$11,576	$43,101
3							
4	Expenses						
5	Salaries		$4,400	$4,400	$4,400	$4,400	$17,600
6	Commissions		600	630	662	695	2,586
7	Payroll taxes		500	503	506	509	2,019
8	Rent		1,350	1,350	1,350	1,350	5,400
9	Total expenses		$6,850	$6,883	$6,918	$6,954	$27,605
10							
11	Net income		$3,150	$3,617	$4,107	$4,622	$15,497

Illustration 3.5   *Total Column Cleaned Up*

Subtraction Error?

Notice that there appears to be a subtraction error in cell G11. Why does cell G11 display $15,497 when in fact $43,101 minus $27,605 equals $15,496? Did the program make a mistake? The answer is no. This is the same type of error discussed in Lesson 2 where formatting a cell may result in some rounding differences when it comes to screen presentation of values. This "error" can be eliminated with the ROUND function. See Appendix A.

SAVE YOUR MODEL

Excel saves the active cell's current position when a file is saved. It is a good habit to move the active cell back to cell A1 before saving so that you always know exactly where you are when you open the file again. Move to cell A1 now.

Since you have made many changes to your model, please use the **Save As** command (**File** menu) now to save your updated financial plan using the file name **Plan3**.

MOVING DATA

In addition to being able to copy data, Excel also allows you to move data. Moving data is different than copying data. Copying data involves making a copy of the original data and then placing the copy at another location on the worksheet. Moving data involves picking up the original data and then placing it somewhere else on the worksheet.

There are several ways that you can move data. Two ways will be discussed here: (1) using the mouse to drag and drop and (2) using the Cut and Paste commands or buttons.

Moving Data with the Mouse (Drag and Drop)

To demonstrate the first type of move, suppose that you want to move some of the quarterly headings and consulting fee projections (range A1 to G2) to a section of the worksheet below the quarterly net income figures (range A13 to G14). Use the following steps to do this:

1. Select the range A1 to G2.

2. Position the mouse pointer on the bottom border of this range so the mouse pointer changes to an arrow.

3. Press and hold down the left mouse button.

4. Drag the dashed outline to the range A13 to G14 and then release the left mouse button. In a flash the move is completed.

	A	B	C	D	E	F	G
1							
2							
3							
4	Expenses						
5	Salaries		$4,400	$4,400	$4,400	$4,400	$17,600
6	Commissions		600	630	662	695	2,586
7	Payroll taxes		500	503	506	509	2,019
8	Rent		1,350	1,350	1,350	1,350	5,400
9	Total expenses		$6,850	$6,883	$6,918	$6,954	$27,605
10							
11	Net income		$3,150	$3,617	$4,107	$4,622	$15,497
12							
13			1st Qtr	2nd Qtr	3rd Qtr	4th Qtr	Total
14	Consulting fees		$10,000	$10,500	$11,025	$11,576	$43,101

It is important to note that all formulas affected by a move are automatically updated by Excel. For instance, the formula in cell D11 now reads =D14-D9, whereas it used to read =D2-D9.

Let's undo this move now. Click the **Undo** button on the toolbar.

Undo

Moving Data with Cut and Paste

The Cut and Paste commands (or buttons) can be used to move cells to new locations. The process is straightforward. You first select a cell or range of cells to be moved. Then you click the Cut button on the toolbar. Finally, select the range where the data is to be moved and click the Paste button. As before, all formulas will be automatically updated. This method will not be demonstrated.

Cut

Paste

DELETING AND INSERTING COLUMNS, ROWS, AND SHEETS

Edit Delete Command

The Edit Delete command has four options. The options to shift cells left or shift cells up are used to delete the cells you specify and the surrounding cells shift to fill in the space. Selecting Entire Column will delete an entire column from the worksheet. Selecting Entire Row will delete an entire row from the worksheet.

To demonstrate this command, let's delete column B from the worksheet. This is an ideal column to delete because there are no entries in it. Move the active cell to any cell in column B (the row doesn't matter), select the **Edit Delete** command, select the **Entire Column** button, and then select **OK**. Your computer screen will look like Illustration 3.6 when you have deleted Column B.

	A	B	C	D	E	F	G
1		1st Qtr	2nd Qtr	3rd Qtr	4th Qtr	Total	
2	Consulting fees	$10,000	$10,500	$11,025	$11,576	$43,101	
3							
4	Expenses						
5	Salaries	$4,400	$4,400	$4,400	$4,400	$17,600	
6	Commissions	600	630	662	695	2,586	
7	Payroll taxes	500	503	506	509	2,019	
8	Rent	1,350	1,350	1,350	1,350	5,400	
9	Total expenses	$6,850	$6,883	$6,918	$6,954	$27,605	
10							
11	Net income	$3,150	$3,617	$4,107	$4,622	$15,497	

Illustration 3.6   *Old Column B Is Deleted*

Instantly, the column is deleted and the remaining columns containing the quarterly financial plan data all shift one column to the left. Before the deletion, the 1st Qtr figures were in column C but now they are in column B. All formulas affected by the deletion are automatically updated by the program. For instance, the for-mula for 2nd Qtr Net income has been changed from =D2-D9 to =C2-C9 (a dif-ference of one column).

Once a column or row is deleted, an easy way to restore it is to use the Edit Undo command, but this only works if no additional commands have been entered since the deletion. Otherwise, the only way to recover from a mistaken deletion is to retype everything. Yuck!

Insert Command

Suppose you wish to insert a title at the top of the financial plan. Right now there is no place at the top of the worksheet to do this. Let's solve this problem by inserting four new rows at the top of the worksheet. To do this, move to any cell in row 1 (the column does not matter) and select a range that extends from row 1 to row 4 (A1 to A4, for example, as shown in Illustration 3.7). Now select the **Rows** command (**Insert** menu) and instantly four new rows are inserted at the top of the financial plan.

	A	B	C	D	E	F	G
1							
2							
3							
4							
5		1st Qtr	2nd Qtr	3rd Qtr	4th Qtr	Total	
6	Consulting fees	$10,000	$10,500	$11,025	$11,576	$43,101	
7							
8	Expenses						
9	Salaries	$4,400	$4,400	$4,400	$4,400	$17,600	
10	Commissions	600	630	662	695	2,586	
11	Payroll taxes	500	503	506	509	2,019	
12	Rent	1,350	1,350	1,350	1,350	5,400	
13	Total expenses	$6,850	$6,883	$6,918	$6,954	$27,605	
14							
15	Net income	$3,150	$3,617	$4,107	$4,622	$15,497	

Illustration 3.7   *Inserting Four New Rows*

Again, all formulas affected by an insertion are automatically updated by the program. For instance, the 2nd Qtr Net income figure used to be calcu-lated by the formula =C2-C9 but now the formula has been updated to read =C6-C13 (a difference of four rows).

Now enter **Fast Track Inc.** in cell B2 and **Financial Plan** in cell B3. To enlarge the font size for these titles, select the range B2 to B3, click the **Font size** drop-down box, and then select **14**. Next, click the **Bold** and **Italic** buttons on the toolbar. Finally, select the range B2 to E2 (note: this is E2, not E3) and click the **Merge and Center** button on the toolbar. This centers Fast Track,

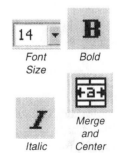

Font
Size

Bold

Italic

Merge
and
Center

Inc. across these columns of your worksheet. The Merge and Center command only works on one row at a time.

Now, repeat this step to center the entry in cell B3 to E3 across columns.

Finally, let's add a border around the company name and statement title. Select the range B2 to E3, click the **Borders** drop-down arrow on the toolbar, and click the **outline** border shown in the lower right corner of the option box. A solid border now outlines the title. See Illustration 3.8. Plan3 is done!

Borders

	A	B	C	D	E	F	G
1							
2		*Fast Track Inc.*					
3		*Financial Plan*					
4							
5		1st Qtr	2nd Qtr	3rd Qtr	4th Qtr	Total	
6	Consulting fees	$10,000	$10,500	$11,025	$11,576	$43,101	
7							
8	Expenses						
9	Salaries	$4,400	$4,400	$4,400	$4,400	$17,600	
10	Commissions	600	630	662	695	2,586	
11	Payroll taxes	500	503	506	509	2,019	
12	Rent	1,350	1,350	1,350	1,350	5,400	
13	Total expenses	$6,850	$6,883	$6,918	$6,954	$27,605	
14							
15	Net income	$3,150	$3,617	$4,107	$4,622	$15,497	

Illustration 3.8   *Plan3 is Done!*

SAVE AND PRINT YOUR WORK

Once again it is time to save your financial plan. Move to cell A1 and click the **Save** button on the toolbar to save Plan3 again. Then, click the **Print** button to print out your financial plan.

Save

Print

WHAT-IF ANALYSIS

You were introduced to what-if analysis in Lessons 1 and 2, but this expanded model provides a basis for more meaningful exposure to this topic. Notice that total net income for the year is $15,497. What would it be if 1st Qtr consulting fees were $11,000 instead of $10,000? Try it and see. Enter **11000** in cell B6. Notice that the model recalculates and total net income for the year is now $19,522.

This model will answer all sorts of what-if questions: What is net income for the 4th Qtr if 1st Qtr consulting fees are $12,538? What are total expenses for the year if 1st Qtr consulting fees are $9,000? Try these out and check your answer below.

Now try this backwards what-if question: What do 1st Qtr consulting fees need to be in order to have net income for the year equal at least $20,000? Answer this by trying different values in cell B6 until you get net income for the year to equal at least $20,000. Check your answer at the end of the lesson.[1]

Although this financial plan allows you to answer numerous what-if questions, only 1st Qtr consulting fees (cell B6) can be easily changed. It would require many steps to change the quarterly growth rate to 7%, the payroll tax rate to 15%, or rent to $1,500. Models that you use to perform what-if analysis should be designed so that all important inputs can be easily changed. Review the file AAPEX in Appendix C to see how all the inputs in that model have been placed into a Data Section so that they can be changed without having to redo formulas each time. This is an excellent design for what-if analysis.

MOUSE SHORTCUT

When you are working in Excel, pressing the right mouse button displays a list of shortcut commands. Many of the commands used in this lesson are found on the list. These commands will change as you move the mouse over different areas and objects in the worksheet.

FINAL COMMENT

In this lesson you were exposed to numerous commands that enable you to expand and modify worksheets to better suit your needs. The Fast Track financial plan is now in a very functional and presentable state.

Now that you are done with Lesson 3, close this file *without* saving any of the changes that have been made to it during the what-if analysis. You want to keep the original financial plan numbers intact. To do this, select the **Exit** or **Close** command (**File** menu) and then select **No** when you are asked to save changes in Plan3.

Lesson 4 will introduce you to several features of Excel that you may find helpful as you begin designing your own spreadsheet models in the future.

---

[1]The answers to the questions are $7,366, $27,320, and $11,119 respectively.

Lesson 4

TOP TEN LIST

LEARNING OBJECTIVES

In this lesson, you will learn to:

- Establish and change global settings
- Use special date formats
- Automatically fill ranges with sequential values
- Establish standard column widths
- Use "Accounting" underlines
- Protect files and cells from alteration
- Name cells and ranges to clarify formulas
- Freeze columns and rows on the screen
- Use multiple sheets
- Add artwork to worksheets

BEFORE BEGINNING

This lesson consists of ten important skill areas for power users of Excel. They are not in any particular order. While you are encouraged to work through the entire lesson, each section is independent and may be completed without regard to any other section. Save any of the work you want as Plan4.

You should have the workbook Plan3 available on your file diskette, hard drive, or network. To begin this lesson, the Excel program should be started and a blank worksheet should be on your screen (use the File New command if necessary). Do not open the Plan3 workbook yet.

1. GLOBAL SETTINGS

Global settings are commands that affect the entire workbook. Five important global settings are mentioned in this lesson.

Setting a Global Numeric Format

Click **Style** (**Format** menu). The dialog box that pops up shows all of the styles used throughout the workbook. There are occasions where you may wish to change these styles. For example, suppose you wanted all numeric entries on the worksheet to be entered in the Currency style (dollars and cents). To demonstrate this, click the word **Number** and then click the **Modify** button. Next, on the Number tab select **Currency** style, set it for **2** decimal places, and click **OK** twice. Now, all numbers entered subsequently on the worksheet will be in dollars and cents. Go ahead and experiment with this now.

Before moving on to the next section, reset the Number format to **General**.

Setting a Global Font

This option allows you to alter your font style and size of all entries throughout the worksheet. Use the same process as setting a global numeric format. Choose **Style** (**Format** menu) and click the **Font** tab. Experiment with this if you wish. Before moving on to the next section, reset the font and size to **Arial 10**.

If you want to make the global font change permanent, not only for this worksheet but for all future worksheets, select **Options** (**Tools** menu), and on the General tab choose your new standard font.

Eliminating Display of Zero Values

Sometimes spreadsheet models contain cells with lots of formulas that have zero value because of the current data entered in other cells. Rather than have a model print columns of zeros, you can suppress the display of zeros. To do this, select **Options** (**Tools** menu), and on the View tab deselect the **Zero values** box. Try it out if you wish.

Tools Options Edit Cell Selector Movement

Normally, when you enter data in a cell and press the ENTER key, the cell selector moves down to the next row. Many people find this irritating because they want to continue working in that same cell (to format it, to perform what-if analysis, etc.) without having to go back to it each time they press ENTER. They do not want the cell selector to move down automatically. Automatic cell selector movement can be eliminated by selecting **Options** (**Tools** menu), and on the Edit tab deselect the **Move Selection after Enter** box.

Activating the HOME Key

Moving the active cell to cell A1 is a common occurrence. In Excel, the normal shortcut to do this is to use the CTRL+HOME keys in combination. All other spreadsheet programs allow you to simply press the HOME key. To choose this option in Excel, select **Options** (**Tools** menu), and on the Transition tab click the **Transition Navigation Keys** box. Checking this box also activates the Tab keys.

2. ENTERING DATES

Many worksheets use calendar dates as a part of labels, and some use them as values (e.g., to calculate the number of days from today until Halloween, etc.).

Entering a date as a label is easy if you begin with a letter or an apostrophe. Excel is also smart enough to recognize certain entries as dates by the way you type them in. For practice, enter **10-31-03** in cell A1. Type **July 4, 2003** in cell B1. You will notice that Excel puts these dates into its own format.

There are three advantages of entering a recognizable date. One is that there are many formatting options available for dates. Move the cell selector to cell A1 and select **Cells** (**Format** menu). Click the **Number** tab and notice the various date formats it uses. Try them out.

A second advantage is that you can do some mathematical operations with the dates. How many days are there from the Fourth of July to Halloween? To find out, enter the formula **=A1-B1** in cell C1. You have to change the number format of cell C1 before you can see the answer (select **Cells** [**Format** menu] and click on the **General** category).

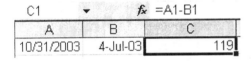

The third advantage is discussed in the next section.

There are several functions specifically designed to assist in the development of models where dates (or time) are an important element. Some of the more important ones are discussed in Appendix A.

3. AUTOFILL (THE FILL HANDLE)

You were introduced to the fill handle in Lesson 3. It can be used to copy formulas and to fill ranges with sequential values. The standard increment is 1. For example, you began with the value $4,400 in cell C5. When you used the fill handle, it put $4,401, $4,402, and $4,403 in cells D5, E5, and F5, respectively. It also works with dates; again, the standard increment is 1 (day).

If you enter two values or dates at the beginning of a range, Excel is programmed to recognize the increment between them and to complete the remaining entries in the range automatically.

For example, type the values **2** and **5** in cells C1 and C2, respectively and then use the mouse to select the range C1 to C2. Next, position the mouse over the small black box located in the lower right corner of cell C2 (called the fill handle), until the pointer becomes a black cross shape. Drag the fill handle down to cell

C5 and then release the mouse button. Instantly, the cells fill up the range with a beginning value of 2 and an increment of 3.

For another example, enter **10/31/03** in cell A1 and **11/30/03** in cell A2. Next, select the range A1 to A2 and drag the fill handle down to cell A5. The range fills with all the month-end dates out to 2/29/04. This example also demonstrates the importance of using a recognizable date format because if these dates were initially entered in an unfamiliar form, Excel would not know what to do. Proper date formats were mentioned in the "Entering Dates" section above.

	A	B	C
1	10/31/2003		2
2	11/30/2003		5
3	12/31/2003		8
4	1/31/2004		11
5	2/29/2004		14

4. UNIFORM COLUMN WIDTHS

Occasionally you may develop a new worksheet where, because of all your experimentation, every column is a different width. If you want to standardize the width of columns containing similar data, you can grab the column borders and try to visually even out the column widths. You may find it difficult to get uniform column widths by sight alone. Where you want more precise column width settings, use the **Column** command (**Format** menu), and select **Width**. This tells you the width of the column where the active cell is, and it allows you to reset it. The standard width of a cell is generally 8.43 when the font is Arial size 10. Try it out!

5. ACCOUNTING UNDERLINES

There are three types of underlining that are in common use: regular underlines, accounting underlines, and bottom borders. An example of the appearance of each is shown below.

May	June	May	June	May	June
Regular Underline		Accounting Underline		Bottom Borders	

The *regular underline* extends only under the data in each cell. The *accounting underline* extends almost all the way across each cell. This type of gapped underline is frequently used in financial reports because it visually breaks up data into distinct columns. The *bottom border* is a solid line drawn all the way across the bottom of the cells.

There are restrictions on where the accounting underlines can be used. In cells that contain values, they can only be used if the cells are in the Accounting number format.

To demonstrate, enter the word **May** in cell D8 and center it in the cell. Next, enter **10,000** in cell D10. Then follow these steps:

1. With the cell selector in cell D8, click the **Underline** button. This puts a regular underline under the word.

May

Underline

2. With the cell selector in cell D8, select **Cells** (**Format** menu) click the **Font** tab. In the Underline text box, select **Single Accounting**, and then click **OK**. This puts an accounting underline across the cell.

May

3. With the cell selector in cell D10, click the **Underline** button. This puts a regular underline under the number.

10,000

4. With the cell selector in cell D10, select **Cells** (**Format** menu) and click the **Font** tab. In the Underline text box, select **Single Accounting**, and then click **OK**. Surprise! What you see is a regular underline, not an accounting one. This is because D10 is a value cell and it has not yet been put into the Accounting number format.

10,000

5. With the cell selector in cell D10, select **Cells** (**Format** menu) and click the **Number** tab. In the Category text box, select **Accounting**, and then click **OK**. Now you will see the accounting underline in that cell.

$ 10,000

Bottom line: Accounting underlines can be used for text and for values expressed in the Accounting number format. Prior planning about this will help!

6. CELL AND WORKSHEET PROTECTION

Open the workbook Plan3 now if it is not already on your screen. Your financial plan worksheet is currently unprotected, meaning that the contents of any cell can be changed. You may, however, protect your worksheet or certain portions of it from change, accidental or otherwise. This is accomplished with the Tools Protection and the Format Cells Protection commands.

Let's work through an example to see how these commands are used. You could protect the entire financial plan worksheet, but this would prevent you from performing what-if analysis or from changing any other aspect of the model. So, the first step before protecting a file is to identify which cells you want to leave unlocked. On your model, the only cell you have changed over and over is cell B6. All the other cells contain text, formulas, and values that could be protected.

To identify cell B6 as a cell you want to leave unlocked, move to cell B6, select the **Cells** command (**Format** menu), and click the **Protection** tab. Deselect the

"Locked" check box and click **OK**. Next, select the **Protection** command (**Tools** menu). Choose the **Protect Sheet** option and then click **OK** (you could enter a password if you want). Your worksheet is now protected. The only cell that can be changed is B6. Try to enter something in some other cell. If you have done this properly, you should be able to enter data in cell B6.

Before moving on to the next section, the model *must be unprotected*. Select the **Protection** command (**Tools** menu), and choose the **Unprotect Sheet** option.

The current protection settings for a workbook are saved when the file is saved. If you wish to save this file, use the **Save As** command (**File** menu), and name the file **Plan46**.

7. CREATING NAMES FOR CELLS AND RANGES

Open the workbook Plan3 now if it is not already on the screen. As mentioned in Lesson 1, it is possible to give a cell or range of cells a descriptive name so that you can use the name to indicate the cell or range rather than having to enter the cell addresses. Names are saved when the workbook is saved.

Name Conventions

There are several name conventions of which you should be aware. For example, the first character in a name must be a letter or an underscore. Names may not contain any spaces or punctuation other than periods or underscores. Excel does not distinguish between uppercase and lowercase letters in names. Additionally, names should not look like cell addresses (i.e., B12), function names, key names, or macro command keywords.

Name Demonstration

To demonstrate this command, move the cell pointer to cell B6 and then click in the **Name** box to highlight the "B6" cell reference.

1.   Type the name **FEES** and then press **ENTER**.

2.   Move the cell pointer to cell B13 and click the **Name** box.

3.   Type the name **EXPENSES** and then press **ENTER**.

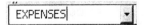

Now, any time you wish to do something to either of these cells, you can indicate the cells by entering FEES or EXPENSES instead of the cell addresses.

Additionally, naming these two cells makes the formula in cell B15 easier to understand. To demonstrate this, move to cell B15 and enter **=FEES-EXPENSES**. Now even a casual user of this financial plan would understand that the value in cell B15 is derived by subtracting total expenses from consulting fees. This method of documenting and clarifying formulas is particularly helpful with long and complex models.

Names can be used with single cells or with a range of cells. Names are automatically updated for insertions, deletions, and moves.

The F5 Key and the Name Box Drop-Down Arrow

Another benefit to using names is that they make it easier to move around the worksheet using either the Name box drop-down arrow or the F5 (GOTO) key. Pressing the F5 key allows you to move the cell pointer to a specific location on the worksheet by specifying a name as the destination.

Clicking the Name box drop-down arrow is an even quicker way of moving the cell pointer to a specific location on the worksheet. To demonstrate, click the **Name** box drop-down arrow to display a list of the two range names you just created. Now click **FEES** and watch the cell pointer jump to cell B6.

Range names can be deleted by selecting Name (Insert menu) Define Delete. Range names are saved when the workbook is saved. If you wish to save this file, use the **Save As** command (**File** menu), and name the file **Plan47**.

8. KEEPING CERTAIN COLUMNS AND ROWS ALWAYS ON THE SCREEN

Open the file Plan3 now if it is not already on the screen. In Excel, the Window Freeze Panes command allows you to freeze a row or column (or both) in place so that it always stays on the screen no matter where the cell pointer is. As you can imagine, this command is very handy with a large worksheet since you can always keep certain column or row headings on the screen.

To demonstrate this command, move the cell pointer to cell B6, select the **Freeze Panes** command (**Window** menu). This freezes column A and rows 1-5 on the screen. To confirm this, move the cell pointer to column M or further and note that column A is still displayed on the screen.

	A	D	E	F	C
1					
2		ack Inc.			
3		al Plan			
4					
5		3rd Qtr	4th Qtr	Total	
6	Consulting fees	$ 11,025	$ 11,576	$43,101	
7					

Move back to cell B6 and then down to row 25 or further and notice that rows 1-5 are still displayed on the screen.

These are examples of what both a column freeze and a row freeze looks like. If you wanted either a column freeze or a row freeze but not both, you would click the row header or column header before using the Freeze Panes command (Window menu).

If you wish to save this workbook, use the **Save As** command (**File** menu), and name the file **Plan49**.

Before you go on to the next section, be sure to eliminate the frozen titles that you have. To do this, select the **Unfreeze Panes** command (**Window** menu).

9. WORKING WITH SHEETS

Open the file Plan3 now if it is not already on the screen. Workbooks may consist of several worksheets. This section will demonstrate some simple mechanics of using multiple sheets. The worksheet tabs at the bottom of the worksheet window allow you to move quickly between different worksheets in a workbook. To demonstrate, click the tab for Sheet2. Now click the tab for Sheet3. That's all there is to it.

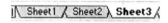

Adding, Moving, and Deleting Sheets

Additional worksheets can be added. With Sheet3 still selected, click **Worksheet** (**Insert** menu) and a new Sheet4 is inserted between Sheet2 and Sheet3.

Sheet1 Sheet2 **Sheet4** Sheet3

Use the mouse button to grab the tab for Sheet3 and move it between Sheet2 and Sheet4. Now all sheets are in numerical order.

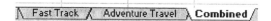

Sheets can be deleted using the **Delete Sheet** command (**Edit** menu). Select Sheet4 and delete it now.

Naming Sheets

Just like range names and file names, worksheets can be given more descriptive names. To demonstrate, double-click the Sheet1 tab, type **Fast Track**, and press **ENTER**. Use the same process to name Sheet2 **Adventure Travel** and Sheet3 **Combined**.

Copy and Paste

Suppose you want to make a projection for Consulting fees for Adventure Travel similar to the one you made for Fast Track. Just as you used Copy and Paste on one worksheet, you can also use it between sheets in a workbook. To demonstrate, go to the Fast Track sheet, select the range A1 to F6, click the **Copy** button, click the **Adventure Travel** sheet tab, and with the cell pointer in cell A1, click the **Paste** button. The column width for column A does not carry over, but everything else should. Make the following four changes to this worksheet: (1) widen column A, (2) change cell B2 to **Adventure Travel**, (3) change cell A6 to **Commissions**, and (4) change cell B6 to **$8,800**. Easy!

Copy

Paste

	A	B	C	D	E	F
1						
2						
3						
4						
5		1st Qtr	2nd Qtr	3rd Qtr	4th Qtr	Total
6	Commissions	$8,800	$ 9,240	$ 9,702	$ 10,187	$37,929
7						

Cells B2:E3: **Adventure Travel Financial Plan**

If you ever want to copy an entire worksheet, click the top left corner box of the worksheet (between column A and row 1). This action selects the entire worksheet. Then click the Copy button, select another sheet, and click the Paste button.

Multiple Sheet Formulas

Suppose you now want to prepare a combined report for fees and commissions in the 1st Quarter. Click the **Combined** sheet tab and enter **Consolidated Total** in cell A1. Next, move to cell C1, type = (equal sign), click the **Fast Track** tab, click cell B6, type + (plus sign), click the **Adventure Travel** tab, click cell B6, and press **ENTER**. The combined total ($18,800) now appears in cell C1. Not very elegant, but you get the idea.

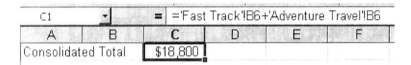

C1	▾	=	='Fast Track'!B6+'Adventure Travel'!B6		
A	B	**C**	D	E	F
Consolidated Total		$18,800			

You've barely scratched the surface on using multiple sheets, but you certainly have enough information now to develop some sophisticated consolidated reports. See the spreadsheet model called SUMMARY in Appendix C for a simple example.

If you wish to save this workbook, use the **Save As** command (**File** menu), and name the file **Plan410**.

10. ARTWORK

Open the file Plan3 now if it is not already on the screen. It is possible to add lines, arrows, geometric shapes, freehand drawings, fancy text, clip art, and other objects to a worksheet. You can add a gazillion colors and patterns as well. Charts and graphs can also be added, but that's covered in the next lesson.

	A	B	C	D	E	F	G	H
2			*Fast Track Inc.*					
3			*Financial Plan*					
4								
5			1st Qtr	2nd Qtr	3rd Qtr	4th Qtr	Total	
6	Consulting fees		$10,000	$10,500	$11,025	$11,576	$43,101	
7								
8	Expenses							
9	*Salaries*		$4,400	$4,400	$4,400	$4,400	$17,600	
10	*Commissions*		600	630	662	695	2,586	
11	*Payroll taxes*		500	503	506	509	2,019	
12	*Rent*		1,350	1,350	1,350	1,350	5,400	
13	Total expenses		$6,850	$6,883	$6,918	$6,954	$27,605	
14								
15	Net income		$3,150	$3,617	$4,107	$4,622	$15,497	

The three quickest places to go for artwork are covered in this section.

Format Cells Patterns

Select your cells and go for color and patterns. Use the Border, Font, and Alignment options as well.

View Toolbars Drawing

This activates the Drawing toolbar. Lots of shapes, shadows, and word art are available with the Drawing toolbar (Excel 2000 version shown below). The Drawing toolbar can also be activated with the Drawing button.

Drawing

Insert Picture (or Insert Objects)

These commands allow you to insert clip art, pictures, scans, sound, and video.

Experiment!

Feel free to experiment as much as you wish. If you want, see if you can recreate the artwork above. The star and checkmark come from Insert Picture ClipArt in Excel 2000. The color in lines 6, 13, and 15 and the pattern in the title box come from Format Cells Patterns. The drop shadow behind the title box comes from the Shadow button on the Drawing toolbar. Zowie comes from the WordArt button on the Drawing toolbar.

As you experiment, you will probably make many mistakes. Rest assured that objects can be deleted, moved, or resized easily after they are initially drawn. And remember that Undo button!

When you are done, print and save your work if you wish. Use the **Save As** command (**File** menu) to save your file as **Plan411**.

Lesson 5

CHARTS

LEARNING OBJECTIVES

In this lesson, you will learn to:

- Create charts based on data in the worksheet
- Save a chart
- Perform what-if analysis with a chart
- Select, move, size, copy, and delete a chart
- Print a chart
- Change the current chart type
- Edit and enhance a chart
- Use Chart Sheets

BEFORE BEGINNING

In this lesson you are going to create some charts. To begin, Excel should be started and the file Plan3 (created in Lesson 3) should be open on your screen.

ABOUT CHARTS IN EXCEL

A chart is basically a graphical representation of the data that you have in your worksheet. Charts are a very important means of communicating information because they allow you to visually examine trends and relationships that exist in the data.

Most charts in Excel have the following basic elements: title, y-axis, y-axis title, x-axis, x-axis title, plot, and legend. In Excel, the y-axis is called the Value axis and the x-axis is called the Category axis. These items are depicted in Illustration 5.1.

Excel makes it very easy for you to create charts on your screen and to print them on a printer. In most cases, charts can be created with a drag and a couple clicks of the mouse. Elements of a chart can be easily modified by the creator.

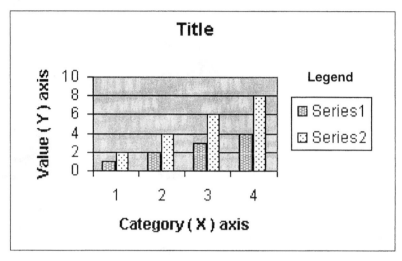

Illustration 5.1   *Basic Chart Elements*

CREATING CHARTS IN EXCEL

To demonstrate the creation of a chart, select the range A5 to E6, click the **Chart Wizard** button, and then click the **Finish** button. Bingo! A chart is immediately drawn. It can't get much easier than that! See Illustration 5.2.

Chart Wizard

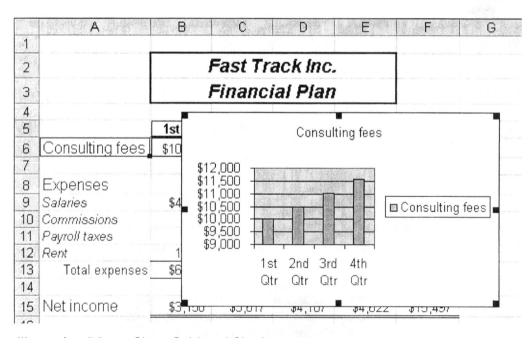

Illustration 5.2   *Chart: Quick and Simple*

You can easily change the chart type from a column graph to another style (line, pie, 3D bar, etc.). A couple clicks or drags lets you resize the chart, move it, copy it, and delete it. You can edit the chart, change the fonts, add color, and other visual effects. It is all pretty simple and straightforward. In fact you could probably end this lesson right now and use what you've just learned (with a little experimenting) to create many attractive charts on your own.

But why experiment on your own when you can take a short, guided tour? That's what this lesson is all about. To begin, press the **DELETE** key to delete the chart you just created. If that doesn't work, close the file Plan3 (without saving it) and then reopen it.

In the chart you just drew, only one data series was plotted: Consulting fees. When you select a range of data to chart, Excel treats each row or column of data in the range as separate data series. Each data series represents a set of values that will be plotted on the chart. Now let's create a new, fancier chart for Fast Track Inc., plotting more than one data series.

Chart Wizard

To demonstrate charting multiple data series, use the mouse to select the range A5 to E6. Next hold down the CTRL key and use the mouse to select a second range A9 to E12. Then click the **Chart Wizard** button. The Chart Wizard guides you through four steps.

Step 1 (Chart Type) allows you to select the chart type. Go ahead and experiment with different chart types. To view the results of each selection, click the button that says "Press and hold to view sample."

The remaining illustrations in this section use the Column chart (upper left corner sub-type). To make sure your charts look like those in this book, select this chart type and sub-type (see Illustration 5.3) before going to Step 2. Then click **Next** to go to Step 2.

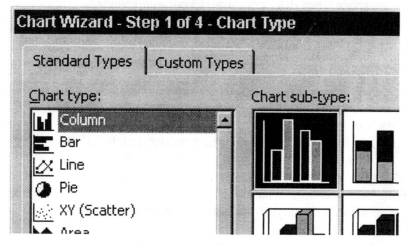

Illustration 5.3   *Chart Wizard Step 1*

Step 2 (Source Data) allows you to select the data ranges to be plotted and to select which categories are to be used on the x-axis. Notice that the chart shown on the Data Range tab has the income and expense categories shown on the x-axis (Category axis) and the four quarters are shown in the legend.

To demonstrate the difference between plotting by columns and plotting by rows, select the **Row** option now (see Illustration 5.4). Notice the graph is redrawn so that the four quarters are on the x-axis (Category axis) and the income and expenses are shown in the legend. Let's use this new orientation for your chart.

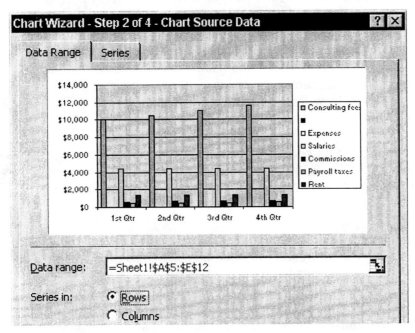

Illustration 5.4   *Chart Wizard Step 2*

When you construct charts, you should be aware of the logic Excel uses. If the range you select to chart has more rows than columns, Excel automatically plots the data series by columns. This is what happened above. If this is not what you had in mind, you can switch the orientation around later, as you just did here.

Click **Next** to go on to Step 3.

Step 3 (Chart Options) allows you to customize the appearance of your chart. For Chart title, enter **Fast Track Inc.** (see Illustration 5.5). If you want to put titles on the x-axis (Category axis) or y-axis (Value axis), you can do that here. Brief descriptions of the other tabs are as follows:

Axes: Custom options for the x- and y-axes
Gridlines: Drawing guidelines vertically or horizontally on your chart
Legend: Placement of the legend
Data Labels: Data values displayed on the chart itself
Data Table: Data arrangement serving as basis for chart

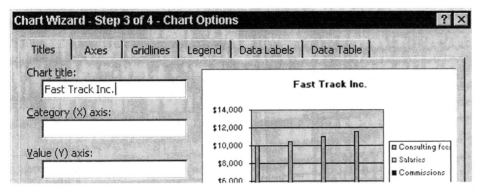

Illustration 5.5   *Chart Wizard Step 3*

Click **Next** to go on to Step 4.

Step 4 (Location) allows you to place the chart on the worksheet (As object in) or on a separate sheet (As new sheet). The second option (As new sheet) will be demonstrated later. For now, select the option to keep **As object in** (see Illustration 5.6) and click **Finish**.

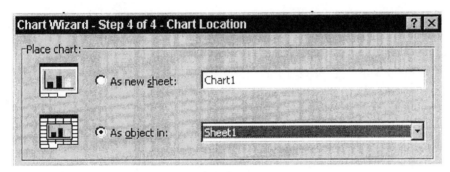

Illustration 5.6   *Chart Wizard Step 4*

When you are done, your chart should appear as in Illustration 5.7 below. Do not be concerned if your y-axis scale is shown in smaller increments.

SAVING A CHART

Now that you have created your chart, you should save it. To save a chart, you simply have to save the file that contains the chart. Do this now. Select the **Save As** command (**File** menu), enter the file name **Plan5** in the file name text box, and then select **OK**. Your chart will now be saved with the rest of the worksheet data.

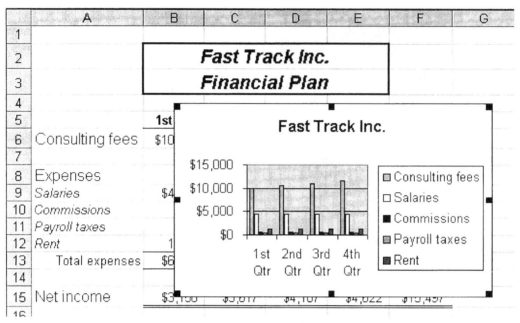

Illustration 5.7   *Chart Wizard Completed*

WHAT-IF ANALYSIS WITH CHARTS

In Excel, charts are dynamic. This means that when you change data in the worksheet, you can immediately see the graphical impact of the change by looking at the chart. The ability to see the effect of changes immediately in the chart can be extremely helpful when performing what-if analysis.

To demonstrate the dynamic link between the worksheet and the chart, you will need to enter a new value in cell B6. If the chart is blocking that cell, click on an open space on the chart and drag it out slightly to the right. Examine the chart and then enter **5000** in cell B6. Examine the chart again and note how the chart has been redrawn to reflect the new value for 1st Qtr consulting fees. Feel free to experiment with other values in cell B6. Reset it to **$10,000** when done.

WORKING WITH CHARTS AS A WHOLE

Charts can be altered or modified after they are created. You can think of a chart as very fancy artwork (covered in Lesson 4). In fact, after you create a chart, you can work with the chart the same way you do with other drawn objects. Charts may be altered using the Chart menu, the Format and Insert menus, the Chart toolbar, or they can be directly edited by pointing at objects within the chart itself and clicking once or twice. A brief summary of some important tasks is presented below.

Selecting a Chart

A chart is selected by clicking once in an open area of the chart. When a chart is selected, it has a series of solid black squares positioned around the outside of the chart. These solid black squares are known as handles. If your chart is currently not selected, click it once now to select it. When a chart is selected, the Chart command replaces the Data command in the main menu.

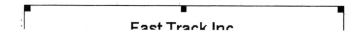

Chart Toolbar

When a chart is selected, the Chart toolbar becomes available. If it is not on your screen now, select **Toolbars** (**View** menu), and click the **Chart** option. If you still do not see it on your screen, chances are it is hidden behind some other toolbar. Turn the other toolbars off until you find the Chart toolbar. See Illustration 5.8. The Chart toolbar offers a few, limited options for modifying the chart. More options are available on the Format menu, Insert menu, and Chart menu. These menu options will be discussed later.

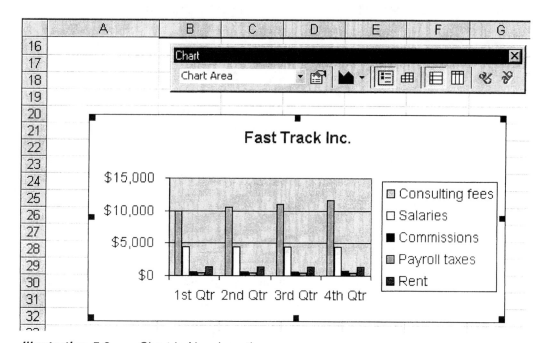

Illustration 5.8   *Chart in New Location*

Moving a Chart

To move a chart, select the chart, position the mouse pointer in any open area within the chart (but not on one of the handles), then press the left mouse button to grab the chart, drag it to a new location, and release the mouse button. Move the chart now so that the upper left corner of the chart is in cell A20.

Sizing a Chart

To resize a chart, select the chart, position the mouse pointer on one of the chart handles so that it changes to a doubled-headed arrow, press the left mouse button to grab the chart border, drag it to the desired size, and then release the mouse button. Resize the chart now so that the lower right corner is in cell G32.

After you are done, your chart should appear as shown in Illustration 5.8.

Copying or Cutting a Chart

Do not do this; just read. To copy a chart, select the chart, click the Copy button or the Cut button, position the cell pointer in the location where you want the copy of the chart to be placed, and then click the Paste button. You may want copies of a chart to show the same data using different chart types, and so forth. Charts can also be pasted to other applications such as word processing programs or presentation programs.

Deleting a Chart

Do not do this; just read. To delete a chart, select the chart and then press the **DELETE** key. You did this at the beginning of the lesson with the first chart you drew.

PRINTING CHARTS

Printing charts in Excel is easy to do. You can print the chart by itself or print it together with the worksheet as they appear on your screen.

To print a chart by itself, simply select the chart and then execute the File Print command as usual. Excel will then print the chart filling an entire page. Let's print your chart now. Click in an open area on your chart to select it, select the **Print** command (**File** menu), and then select **OK**. As with all printing, the Page Setup command (File menu) can be used to modify layout, margins, headers, footers, etc.

You can print the worksheet and the chart together as they appear on your screen. First, deselect the chart by clicking anywhere on the worksheet itself. Then execute the File Print command as usual. Try this now.

CHART TYPES

One of the most obvious ways to change a chart is with the many different chart types that are available. The default chart type in Excel is a two-dimensional column chart. Let's examine other chart types. Begin by selecting the chart. The Chart toolbar appears, but as mentioned earlier, the chart types available on the toolbar are limited.

To look at the full range of chart types available, select **Chart Type** (**Chart** menu). Recall that the Chart command appears in the main menu in place of the Data command only after the chart has been selected. You are presented with a gallery of choices and descriptions. As you click on various chart types, you can press a button to view what the chart will look like with the current data. Try out a few. When you are done, click **OK** or **Cancel**.

CLARIFICATION ON TWO POPULAR CHART TYPES

1. Pie charts display only the first data series (consulting fees in this case). Also, individual slices of a pie can be moved out for visual effect.

2. The XY chart is commonly called a scattergraph. The XY chart requires that the x-axis be values, not labels, otherwise it ends up functioning as a plain old line graph. An example of this would be to plot advertising expense on the x-axis and consulting fees on the y-axis. This would allow you to see what impact advertising had on consulting fees. See Illustration 5.9.

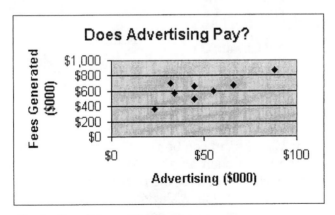

Illustration 5.9   *XY Chart*

EDITING CHARTS

There are many other features available to alter charts and objects within charts, such as titles, legend, and data series. You can add or change colors, patterns, fonts, gridlines, data labels, artwork, and so forth.

As a simple demonstration of this, select the chart. Then click the title Fast Track, Inc., once. You can see by the handles placed around the title that it has been selected.

Select the **Format** command and choose the **Selected Chart Title** option. Three tabs become available for enhancing the title: Patterns, Font, and Alignment. Click on the **Patterns** tab. This tab is divided into two sections: Border and Area. Border can be used to place a border around the title. Click the **Shadow** box.

Area can be used to color or fill the area around the title. To demonstrate this option, click the **Fill Effects** button and pick a pattern on the **Textures** tab. Click **OK** twice. An example of how your chart might appear is shown in Illustration 5.10.

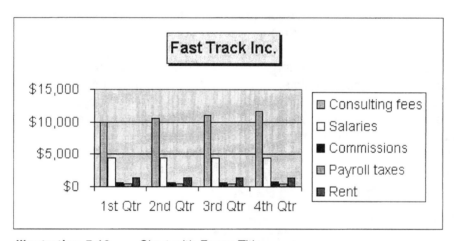

Illustration 5.10   *Chart with Fancy Title*

This is a very simple example of how your chart can be visually enhanced. What you did to the title can also be done to the chart as a whole and to other chart objects. With the extensive options available in Excel, the possibilities are practically limitless. Go ahead and experiment if you wish. You can also use the Drawing toolbar (see Lesson 4) to add geometric shapes, fancy text, and shadows to your chart. Remember the Undo command if you create something you do not like!

A Warning

When creating a chart, always keep in mind that its purpose is to visually communicate information to the user. If the viewer has to struggle to figure out what the chart is illustrating because it is too cluttered, you are defeating the benefit of using a chart.

SAVE YOUR WORK

Since you have made changes to your chart, save your file again under the name **Plan5**. Click the **Save** button.

Save

CHART SHEETS

So far, your chart has been located as an object in the worksheet. It floats above the worksheet and can be moved around to different spots. Charts can also be placed on separate sheets called Chart Sheets. To demonstrate this now, let's move your chart into its own special sheet.

Select the chart. Then choose the **Location** command (**Chart** menu) and pick the **As new sheet** option. Click **OK**. The chart is now on a sheet by itself called Chart1. Click the **Sheet1** tab and notice that only the worksheet itself is there. See Illustration 5.11.

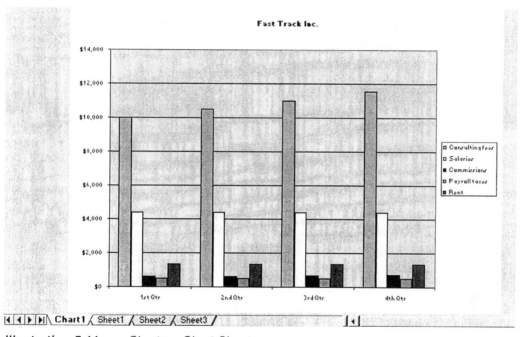

Illustration 5.11   *Chart on Chart Sheet*

CHART DATA TABLES

When you have data in several locations on a worksheet that you wish to plot in a single chart, you may select several ranges at once using the mouse and the CTRL key. However, if the data is too disconnected, the Chart Wizard may have difficulty constructing the chart you want. You may find it easier in these cases to use a separate section of the worksheet to accumulate all the data in one place. If data is placed in a tabular format (neat columns and rows), the Chart Wizard will have little difficulty constructing the chart you want.

FINAL COMMENT

This lesson covered how to create, work with, save, enhance, and print charts. Charts are a very effective means of presenting data, so you are strongly encouraged to continue working with them. Keep in mind that establishing a purpose for your chart is just as important as learning the mechanics of how to create and enhance a chart.

Appendix A
FUNCTIONS FOR BUSINESS

Functions are used to perform special calculations in cells. There are over 200 functions available in Excel, but only the commonly used ones are discussed in this appendix.

Review the section called "Using Functions" in Lesson 2 to refresh your memory on how functions work. That lesson covers entering functions and using the function Help system.

Functions may be linked with standard arithmetic operations and can also be combined with one another. All of the following are legitimate Excel formulas:

```
=D15/VLOOKUP(C12,E4:F9,1)
=SUM(B12:H12)+17
=A17*IF(B1= 0,2,B9)
=IF(H16>12,0,MAX(H2:H9))
```

As a reminder, any time a cell address is used in one of these functions, the cell address can be entered by typing it in or by pointing to it either with the mouse or with the keyboard. Ranges are entered with the beginning and ending cell addresses separated by a colon (e.g., E4:F91).

The following functions are covered in this appendix:

Date:
NOW	gives today's date and time
TODAY	gives today's date

Finance:
FV	future value of an ordinary annuity
PV	present value of ordinary annuity
PMT	periodic loan payment to amortize loan
NPER	number of periods for annuity or amount to reach future value
RATE	interest rate for amount to reach future value

Capital Budgeting:
IRR	internal rate of return
MIRR	IRR with modified reinvestment rate
NPV	net present value

Statistical:

SUM	sum of values in range
AVERAGE	average value in range
COUNT	number of entries
MAX	maximum value in range
MIN	minimum value in range
MEDIAN	median value in range
STDEVP	standard deviation
VARP	variance
FORECAST	predicts next value in series
GROWTH	predicts next several values in series (exponential trend)
TREND	predicts next several values in series (linear trend)
INTERCEPT	computes y-intercept of regression line
SLOPE	computes slope of regression line

Mathematical:

ABS	absolute value
SQRT	square root
RAND	random value
INT	integer portion of value
ROUND	round the value

Logical:

IF	if true, enter one value; if false, enter another
VLOOKUP	look up value in vertical table
HLOOKUP	look up value in horizontal table

Depreciation:

SLN	straight-line
SYD	sum-of-the-years digits
DDB	double-declining balance

Descriptions of each of the above functions are described in alphabetical order on the following pages.

ABS(number)

This function calculates the absolute value of number. Example: =ABS(C11) will return 23.7 if the value in cell C11 is either 23.7 or -23.7.

AVERAGE(list)

This function computes the average value of a specified range or list of cells separated by commas. Examples: =AVERAGE(H12:H20) or =AVERAGE(F4, H4, J4:P4). Also see Appendix C file named CLASS.

COUNT(list)

This function will count the number of nonblank cells in a list of cells separated by commas or in specified ranges. Example: =COUNT(A7,A10,A11:A20). Also see Appendix C file named CLASS.

DDB(cost,salvage,life,period,factor)

This function computes depreciation for an asset using the double-declining balance method. Cost is the cost of the asset, salvage is its estimated salvage value, life is its estimated useful life, and period is the time period for which depreciation is to be computed. For example, =DDB(10000,2000,8,2) would compute depreciation for the second year on an asset that cost $10,000, has an expected useful life of 8 years, and salvage value of $2,000 (answer is $1,875). Entering a value for factor is optional and is only used when changing the depreciation rate.

FORECAST (x,known_y's,known_x's)

This function predicts the next value in a series (e.g., next month's sales based on sales for the last four months) based on a linear trend of existing values. For example, enter the following table on a worksheet:

A1: Month	B1: 1	C1: 2	D1: 3	E1: 4	F1: 5
A2: Sales	B2: 277	C2: 307	D2: 290	E2: 321	

In cell F2 enter the following formula: =FORECAST(F1,B2:E2,B1:E1). The result (327.5) is a linear prediction of sales for month 5. Also, see the TREND function to predict several future values.

FV(rate,nper,pmt,pv,type)

This function computes the future value of an ordinary annuity. Pmt is the amount of each periodic payment and is assumed to occur at the end of the period. Rate is the interest rate per payment, and nper represents the number of payments made. For example, if at the end of each year you put $100 into a savings account earning 5% interest, how much would the account be worth at the end of the fifth year? The formula =FV(.05,5,-100) provides the answer ($552.56).

Entering values for pv and type are optional. If you enter the value 1 for type, Excel will treat the payments as occurring at the beginning of each period.

GROWTH (known_y's,known_x's,new_x's,const)

This function predicts several future values in a series (using an exponential trend) based on past values. This is similar to the TREND function. See the TREND function for an example.

HLOOKUP

See VLOOKUP.

IF(logical_test,value_if_true,value_if_false)

This function allows the program to choose one of two inputs to enter in a cell. If the specified condition is true, input x will be put in the cell. If the condition is false, input y will be entered. An example of how this function can be used is as follows:

    C2: =IF(A8=2,7,9)

This formula states that if the value in cell A8 is equal to 2, enter a 7 in cell C2; if the value in cell A8 is not equal to 2, enter a 9 in cell C2.

The conditions that may be used are as follows:

=	equal to
>	greater than
<	less than
<=	less than or equal to
>=	greater than or equal to
<>	not equal to
AND	logical AND
OR	logical OR
NOT	logical NOT

Here are some acceptable examples:

    B12: =IF(B11>10,B11,B10/D5)
    D23: =IF(A3<A2,D8,"overdrawn")
    D71: =IF(G12>=0,0,SUM(C20:C58))
    F22: =IF(A1=0,B7,IF(A1=1,B8,B9))
    P17: =IF(OR(B7=B8,C15>500),"Credit OK","Credit Not OK")
    E1: =IF(NOT(A2=2),55,66)

Also see Appendix C files named CHECKREG, CHURCH, and PROPERTY.

INT(number)

This function returns the integer portion of number. Example: =INT(27.3) will return the value 27.

INTERCEPT(known_y's,known_x's)

See SLOPE.

IRR(values,guess)

This function will approximate the internal rate of return for a series of cash flows (represented by values in a range of cells). To start the process, you must enter an initial guess (from 0.00 to 1.0) either as a number or as a cell address.

Suppose you wish to evaluate an investment that will cost $200,000 today and will generate $60,000 per year at the end of the first two years and $75,000 per year at the end of the next two years. The projected cash flows are entered in cells B17 through B21 as follows: -$200,000; $60,000; $60,000; $75,000; and $75,000. You want the IRR to be entered in cell C6. Your initial guess is 10%. The formula is as follows:

    C6: =IRR(B17:B21,.1)

The internal rate of return for this investment will show up in cell C6 as 13%. For another example, see Appendix C file named PROPERTY.

MAX(list)

This function returns the maximum value found in specified ranges or a list of cells separated by commas. Example: =MAX(B8:B28). Also see Appendix C file named CLASS.

MEDIAN(list)

This function returns the median value found in specified ranges or a list of cells separated by commas. Example: =MEDIAN(P1:P32).

MIN(list)

This function returns the minimum value found in specified ranges or a list of cells separated by commas. Example: =MIN(C1:C8,C12:C20). Also see Appendix C file named CLASS.

MIRR(values,finance_rate,reinvestment_rate)

This function computes the modified internal rate of return on a range of cash flows. This formula is used when the reinvestment rate is different than the financing rate. Also see IRR.

NOW( )

This function calculates the date and time currently showing on your computer's clock. It is a very useful means of date- or time-stamping worksheets. Excel recalculates the value of NOW each time you recalculate your work and it will show this value when the file is printed. For examples, see Appendix C files named BUPLAN and INVOICE.

NPER(rate,pmt,pv,fv,type)

This function computes the number of compounding periods it would take for an investment (pv) plus periodic payments (pmt) to grow to a future value (fv) if the amounts were invested at a specific interest rate (rate) per period. For example, if $10,000 is invested today at 11% interest compounded annually and $1,000 is added at the end of each year, how many years would it take to grow to $15,000? The formula =NPER(.11,-1000,-10000,15000) provides the answer (2.23 years). Notice that amounts invested are entered as negative numbers.

If no periodic payments are involved and you want to find how long it will take $10,000 to grow to $15,000 at 11% interest, the formula =NPER(.11,0,-10000,15000) provides the answer (3.89 years).

If there is no beginning investment, and you want to find how long it will take $1,000 annual amounts invested at 11% to grow to $15,000, the formula =NPER(.11,-1000,0,15000) provides the answer (9.34 years).

If you enter a value of 1 for Type, Excel will treat the payments (pmt) as occurring at the beginning of the year instead of at the end.

NPV(rate,range)

This function will automatically compute the net present value of annual future cash flows (represented by values in a range of cells) discounted at a specific interest rate (interest). The interest rate may be expressed as a number or as a cell address.

Suppose that an investment's projected future cash inflows at the end of each of the next three years (say, $1,000, $1,800, $2,500) are entered in cells D38, E38, and F38. You wish to compute the present value of these future cash flows using a discount rate of 11%. The result is to be put in cell H14. This will be accomplished by the following formula:

H14: =NPV(.11,D38:F38)

The answer is $4,189.80.

If the discount rate is found in cell B2, one of the following formulas will work:

H14: =NPV(B2,D38:F38) or
H14: =NPV(B2/100,D38:F38) if B2 is an integer

If a cash outlay is necessary at the beginning of the first year to acquire this investment, the cash outlay (found in cell G12) must be subtracted from the formula as follows:

  H14: =NPV(B2,D38:F38)-G12

The initial cash outlay must be handled separately like this any time it occurs at the beginning of the year. This is because NPV treats all payments as occurring at the end of the year.

PMT(rate,nper,pv,fv,type)

This function will compute the periodic payment amount needed to pay back a loan. Pv is the amount borrowed in dollars, rate is the interest rate per payment, and nper is the number of payments to be made. For example, =PMT(.11,10,-100000) would compute the annual payment needed to retire a $100,000 loan at 11% interest over ten years (answer is $16,980.14). If the payments were to be made monthly, the formula should be written as =PMT(.11/12,120,-100000) (answer is $1,377.50).

Fv and type are optional. With type omitted or set to 0, payments are assumed to be made at the end of each period. If payments are made at the beginning of each period, set type to 1 (answer would be $15,297.43). For other examples, see Appendix C files named AMORTIZE and PROPERTY.

PV(rate,nper,pmt,fv,type)

This function computes the present value of an ordinary annuity. Pmt is the amount of each periodic payment, rate is the interest rate per payment, and nper is the number of payments made. For example, =PV(.08,7,-100) would compute the present value of $100 payments to be made at the end of each of the next seven years discounted at an annual rate of 8% (answer is $520.64).

Fv and type are optional. If the payments are being made at the beginning of each period, set type to 1 (answer is $562.29).

RAND( )

This function generates a random value between 0 and 1. Example: =RAND()*5 will generate a random number between 0 and 5. The random value changes each time the worksheet performs a new calculation.

RATE(nper,pmt,pv,fv,type,guess)

This function computes the interest rate per period required to make a present investment (pv) plus periodic payments (pmt) grow to a future value (fv) in a specific number of periods (nper). For example, if $10,000 was invested today with no future periodic payments, what annual interest is required to have it grow to $15,000 in eight years? The formula =RATE(8,0,-10000,15000) provides the answer (5.2%).

Type and guess are optional. Set type to 1 if the periodic payments are made at the beginning of the period rather than at the end.

ROUND(number,num_digits)

This function will round a value to a specified number of decimals. This is particularly useful when a cell formula involves either multiplication with a decimal or any kind of division. For example, if cell D2 contains the formula =ROUND(C2*27.389,2), the computer will round the product of C2*27.389 to two decimal places and enter it in cell D2. =ROUND(C2*27.389,0) will round the product to zero decimal places (an integer).

ROUND is different from the Decrease Decimal button (or Increase Decimal button) because ROUND eliminates all values to the right of the decimal places specified. The Decrease and Increase Decimal buttons change the *appearance* of the values on the screen but do not alter the values in the cells themselves. Using the ROUND function would have eliminated the problems encountered in several tutorial lessons where a column of numbers did not appear to add up correctly because of rounding errors. For example, in Plan3 if all formulas in rows 6, 10, and 11 had used ROUND specifying 0 decimals (e.g., cell B10: =ROUND(C6*.06,0), none of the "subtraction" errors would have occurred. For additional examples see Appendix C files named AMORTIZE, CHECKREG, COSTJOB, and INVOICE.

SLN(cost,salvage,life)

This function computes depreciation for an asset using the straight-line method. Cost is the cost of the asset, salvage is its estimated salvage value, and life is its estimated useful life. For example, =SLN(10000,2000,8) would compute depreciation for an asset that cost $10,000, has an expected useful life of 8 years, and salvage value of $2,000 (answer is $1,000).

SLOPE(known_y's,known_x's)
INTERCEPT(known_y's,known_x's)

These functions are used in linear regression analysis. SLOPE computes the slope for a range of data points that could be plotted on an XY chart (scattergraph). INTERCEPT computes the y-intercept. For example, suppose you want to develop a cost prediction formula for your monthly manufacturing costs. Some costs are fixed and some vary with your production levels. Enter the following production data for the last three months onto a worksheet:

C10:	Manufacturing	D10:	Units
C11:	Costs	D11:	Produced
C12:	$9000	D12:	100
C13:	$28000	D13:	550
C14:	$25000	D14:	375

=INTERCEPT(D12:D14,C12:C14) gives you a y-intercept of $5,755. This represents the fixed costs each month. =SLOPE(D12:D14,C12:C14) computes a slope of $43.64. This is the variable cost per unit produced.

SQRT(number)

This function calculates the square root of number. Example: =SQRT(G55) will compute the square root of the value found in cell G55.

STDEVP(list)

This function calculates the standard deviation of values in specified ranges or a list of cells separated by commas. Example: =STDEVP(F26:F35).

SUM(list)

This function adds the values found in specified ranges or a list of cells separated by commas. Examples: =SUM(A1:A22) or =SUM(A21,A24,A27:A50). See Appendix C for several examples of using this function.

SYD(cost,salvage,life,per)

This function computes depreciation for an asset using the sum-of-the-years digits method. Cost is the cost of the asset, salvage is its estimated salvage value, life is its estimated useful life, and period is the time period for which depreciation is to be computed. For example, =SYD(10000,2000,8,2) would compute depreciation for the second year on an asset that cost $10,000, has an expected useful life of 8 years, and salvage value of $2,000 (answer is $1,555).

TODAY( )

This function shows the current date on your computer. This is exactly like NOW except that it only calculates the date, not the time, too.

TREND (known_y's,known_x's,new_x's,const)

This function predicts several future values in a series (using a linear trend) based on past values. This is similar to the FORECAST function, except that TREND can predict several future values at once. For example, enter on a worksheet the same table used to demonstrate the FORECAST function. Next enter 6, 7, 8 in cells G1, H1, and I1 respectively. Then, to predict the next four month's sales, select the range F2 to I2 and type the following formula (but *do not* press ENTER): =TREND(B2:E2,B1:E1,F1:I1).

Once you've typed the formula, hold down the SHIFT and CTRL keys, and then press ENTER. The array fills with values for the next four months.

The GROWTH function works the same way, but it returns values using an exponential trend.

VARP(list)

This function calculates the variance of values in specified ranges or a list of cells separated by commas. Example: =VARP(G18:G42,G44).

**VLOOKUP(lookup_value,table_array,col_index_num) and
HLOOKUP(lookup_value,table_array,row_index_num)**

These functions allow you to look up a value in a table. They are similar in concept to the IF function, but they allow the program to pick an answer from a whole table of values. VLOOKUP stands for a vertical table (values entered up and down), and HLOOKUP stands for a horizontal table (values entered side by side).

For an example of how the VLOOKUP function works, suppose you are setting up a Excel model to use in tax planning for your clients. As a part of the tax planning program, you want a client's tax bracket to be automatically computed based on his/her taxable income. You obtain the following (hypothetical) information from the Internal Revenue Service:

	Taxable Income	
Over	**But Not Over**	**Tax Bracket**
$ 0	$ 5,000	15%
5,000	12,000	19
12,000	21,000	23
21,000	34,000	28
34,000	60,000	36
60,000	—	50

You can incorporate this tax table into your tax planning model by constructing the following table:

E40:	INCOME	F40:	BRACKET
E41:	0	F41:	15%
E42:	5000	F42:	19%
E43:	12000	F43:	23%
E44:	21000	F44:	28%
E45:	34000	F45:	36%
E46:	60000	F46:	50%

Now assume that the client's taxable income will be computed by your tax model and will be entered in cell G10. You wish to have the client's tax bracket automatically determined by the program and shown in cell G11. The following formula would be used:

G11: =VLOOKUP(G10,E41:F46,2)

The VLOOKUP function searches the leftmost column of the table for the value closest to, but not larger than, the value in cell G10. The program then moves across the row to the column number specified and returns the value of that cell as the answer in cell G11.

As an example, suppose the taxable income value found in cell G10 is $10,000. In evaluating cell G11, the program would jump to cell E41 and begin looking for the value closest to, but not greater than, 10000. The cell containing a value closest to, but not greater than, 10000 is cell E42 (it contains 5000). The program then picks up the corresponding value in column 2 (19%) and enters it in cell G11.

The range of cells entered in the middle of the VLOOKUP formula begins with the top of the leftmost column and ends with the bottom of the last data column. Lookup tables can have many data columns.

For additional examples, see Appendix C files named CLASS and TAXCOMP.

Note the following three things about the VLOOKUP and HLOOKUP functions:

1. If the value being searched for is less than the lowest number in the table, the program will indicate this by returning #NA. In our example, this is what would happen if the value of G10 were less than zero.

2. The table must always be constructed in ascending order.

3. The table may be constructed in rows instead of columns. If rows are used, the HLOOKUP function is utilized. The top row is searched (left to right) and the rows below it contain the values that will be returned.

Appendix B
MODEL-BUILDING HINTS

The term "model building" may sound highly technical and sophisticated, but this is not necessarily the case with spreadsheet models. Although elaborate and complex spreadsheet models can be designed to handle everything from detailed investment analysis to complex engineering applications, spreadsheet models can also be developed to solve simple problems, too. As you saw in the tutorial lessons, the quarterly financial plan was an elementary, yet flexible, model, and it was fairly easy to design and use.

This appendix provides some general recommendations on model-building techniques. Suggestions for constructing and documenting spreadsheet models are stressed. Each time you begin building a model, you may want to review this list.

1. Planning saves time and trouble. Although there are many ways to correct design problems with spreadsheet models (e.g., Insert, Edit Delete, Edit Cut, and Edit Paste), much time will be saved if you lay out a tentative structure for the model on paper before turning the computer on.

    Particular attention should be given to global number formats and text fonts using the Style command (Format menu) (see Lesson 4, part 1). These should be entered on the worksheet before any entries are made. You can always override these settings later (with other Format commands) if specific cells require special formatting or fonts.

2. Use all available resources. When you have a question, don't hesitate to examine other Excel manuals besides this one. Use the Help command within Excel. To registered users, Microsoft's own telephone support line is (425) 635-7070. There are also some helpful websites, too. Limited help is available at Microsoft's website at http://www.microsoft.com. A second interesting website is The Spreadsheet Page at http://j-walk.com/ss.

3. Use cell and range names wherever appropriate to document and clarify the formulas in your model.

4. Document your worksheet. You should design your model so that six months from now you can remember the purpose of the worksheet and how it works.

    a. Choose a file name for your model that is both descriptive and simple. This will help eliminate the frustration associated with selecting incorrect files.

    b. You may wish to put a short, written description of what the model does on the face of the worksheet.

c. Where appropriate, include important instructions and explanatory notes on the face of the worksheet.

d. Clearly indicate on the worksheet the assumptions that underlie any calculations. An easy way to accomplish this is to include a Data Section at the top of the worksheet. The purpose of a Data Section is to isolate all relevant assumptions and variables in one spot on the worksheet. A Data Section should always be given strong consideration since it helps highlight the numerical assumptions of the model, and it facilitates performing what-if analysis.

Without a Data Section, labels, data, and/or formulas are entered directly in the model at their appropriate locations. If new information is provided, the new labels, data, and/or formulas will have to be reentered directly throughout the entire model. This direct-entry model is an acceptable design if the changeable information is data or labels only. It is generally inefficient and cumbersome if the change in data involves revising formulas.

With a Data Section, all of the input data will be placed in one spot on the model, and all formulas in the answer will reference the appropriate cells in the Data Section. If new information is provided, changes are made to the Data Section only. No formulas need to be revised.

Review the printout of the file AAPEX in Appendix C. This is an example of a model using a Data Section. There are four assumptions in the model: January sales are $100, sales growth rate is 2% per month, selling expenses are 60% of sales, and general expenses are $19 per month. Note that the four assumptions of the model are listed in the Data Section, and they are the only cells unprotected. All cells in the Answer Section contain formulas that use cell addresses from the Data Section. Thus, any time you enter new values in the Data Section, the Answer Section recalculates a new answer without having to redo the formulas. As a result of its design, this model is extremely flexible and offers excellent opportunities for performing what-if analysis.

5. Pay attention to alignment and format. Put labels over all columns. Use the currency and accounting formats where appropriate. Use an integer format (no decimal places) where decimal accuracy is not needed. Use standard accounting conventions, such as underlines, double underlines, and accepted abbreviations, whenever appropriate. Use uppercase and lower-case letters just as you would in a handwritten or typed report. Arrange all worksheet input data in either columns or rows, not a combination of both. A visually consistent worksheet is easier to read and reduces the possibility of errors. Your model may perform a sophisticated analysis, but if it is cluttered and difficult to read, no one will appreciate your brilliance.

6. When printing your model, you do not have to print all cells used to calculate your answer. It is a common practice to place scratch pads and tables out of

sight if they clutter up your printout or do not provide useful information to the model user.

7. Beware of being too comprehensive. It may be easy to develop a model that handles a specific set of facts, but it may be difficult to modify that template to encompass other facts and circumstances. Do not always attempt to cover all possibilities with one single model. For example, it may be easier to develop several different depreciation calculation models than it would be to develop a single model that covers all methods.

8. Always keep flexibility in mind. One of the most powerful features of a spreadsheet program is its ability to perform instant recalculations when new data are entered. This ability is enhanced if your models are designed to accept new input without having to alter previously entered formulas. This is another important reason to use a Data Section at the top of the worksheet.

9. Learn to use Copy and Paste. These commands were discussed in Lesson 3. They can be used frequently when setting up many spreadsheet models. It will save much time and trouble once you get used to them, particularly if you understand the difference between relative and absolute references. If you make a mistake when copying, simply do it over. Try it. Practice makes perfect!

10. Don't be afraid to use the functions discussed in Appendix A. The IF function may scare you, but it looks harder than it really is. The IF function can add a great deal of power and flexibility to your models. The same is true of the HLOOKUP and VLOOKUP functions. You can begin to develop very sophisticated spreadsheet models when you learn to use these commands.

11. In general, if you develop a model with a Data Section, you should enter some sample data before preparing your Answer Section. Developing a blank spreadsheet model with correct formulas and format is extremely difficult.

12. Windows-based programs are designed to work together. For example, material from spreadsheet files can be pasted into word processing documents and vice versa. Practice becoming comfortable working with "objects." Remember the clipboard. Remember Copy and Paste.

13. Protect your worksheet from hardware and software failures. Also, protect your worksheet from accidental changes.

    a. Always keep a printout of the model on file. Should you ever lose or destroy a model saved on a disk, you can reconstruct it much faster by looking at a printout of the original.
    b. Keep a backup copy of your model on a disk separate from the one on which you stored the original model.
    c. As you are developing a model, save it on disk at frequent intervals.

d.   Use the Format Cells Protection command and the Tools Options Protect Sheet command to prevent mistaken entry into or erasure of important cells.

e.   When saving your model to a floppy disk, always check the drive light to see that it goes on. After saving a model to the hard drive, always check to make sure that the file was actually saved.

f.   Generally use the File Save As command for saving. The File Save command is dangerous because it is so easy to accidentally overwrite your original file.

FINAL COMMENT

Model building can be simplified and more creative if these suggestions are followed. You are certain to enjoy developing your own spreadsheet models, but don't be surprised if it's harder than it looks!

Appendix C
SAMPLE SPREADSHEET MODELS

These sample spreadsheet models are available for viewing and downloading from South-Western/Thomson Learning website at http://smith.swlearning.com.

FILE NAME: AAPEX

This model demonstrates:

1. A Data Section where changeable data are entered. A Data Section is an effective way of grouping all changeable data in one place.

2. A net income projection with formulas keyed to data from the Data Section.

How to use this model:

1. Enter beginning assumptions in a Data Section (cells F5 to F8) and observe the resulting six-month projections.

2. Change the assumptions as desired.

3. If the presence of rounding errors bothers you, all formulas in the ranges C15 to G15 and B17 to G17 should contain the ROUND function. These are the ranges where decimal values may occur. As an example of using the ROUND function, the formula in cell C15 would be =ROUND(B15*(1+$F6),0). The zero indicates no decimals (i.e., integers).

The basic design features of this model include:

1. Number formats utilized—Currency (0 decimals)
   —Number (0 decimals)
   —Percent (0 decimals)

2. The single and double underlines were created with the Border button.

3. Month headings were aligned using the Center button.

4. Column widths—Column A: 16
   —Columns B through H: 7

5. Unprotected cells—F5 to F8

The key formulas used in this model include (cell reference to left of colon; formula to right of colon):

B15:	=F5	
C15:	=B15*(1+$F6)	Copy to D15:G15
H15:	=SUM(B15:G15)	Copy to H17:H19, H21
B17:	=B15*$F7	Copy to C17:G17
B18:	=$F8	Copy to C18:G18
B19:	=B17+B18	Copy to C19:G19
B21:	=B15-B19	Copy to C21:G21

	A	B	C	D	E	F	G	H
1	File name: AAPEX							
2	Purpose: Net income projection for Aapex Inc. demonstrating the use of a Data Section							
3								
4				Data Section				
5		January sales estimate				$100		
6		Growth rate per month				2%		
7		Selling expense (% of sales)				60%		
8		General expense per month				$19		
9								
10								
11				Aapex Inc.				
12				Net Income Projection				
13								
14		Jan	Feb	Mar	Apr	May	Jun	Total
15	Sales	$100	$102	$104	$106	$108	$110	$631
16								
17	Selling expenses	60	61	62	64	65	66	378
18	General expenses	19	19	19	19	19	19	114
19	Total expenses	$79	$80	$81	$83	$84	$85	$492
20								
21	Net income	$21	$22	$23	$23	$24	$25	$138
22								

FILE NAME: AMORTIZE

This model demonstrates:

1. A Data Section where changeable data are entered. A Data Section is an effective way of grouping all changeable data in one place.

2. A simple Data Section with a lengthy solution.

3. Use of =PMT and =ROUND functions.

How to use this model:

1. Enter loan principal, interest rate, and number of monthly payments in cells E6, E7, and E8, respectively.

2. Change the data input as desired. You will need to lengthen the Amorti- zation Schedule if the number of monthly payments exceeds 48. Do this by copying the formulas in columns B, C, D, E, and F to the extended range using the Fill Handle. Delete rows in the Answer Section if the number of monthly payments is less than 48.

The basic design features of this model include:

1. Number formats utilized—Currency (2 decimals)
    —Number (2 decimals)
    —General
    —Percent (1 decimal)

2. The single and double underlines were created with the Border button.

3. Column widths—Column A: 5
    —Columns B through F: 12

4. Unprotected cells—E6 to E8

The key formulas used in this model include (cell reference to left of colon; for- mula to right of colon):

```
E12: =ROUND(PMT(E7/12,E8,-E6),2)
F16: =E6
C17: =E$12                        Copy to C18:C64
D17: =ROUND(F16*E$7/12,2)         Copy to D18:D64
E17: =C17-D17                     Copy to E18:E64
F17: =F16-E17                     Copy to F18:F64
```

	A	B	C	D	E	F
1	File name: AMORTIZE					
2	Purpose: Loan amortization schedule					
3						
4				Data Section		
5						
6			Loan principal		$100,000.00	
7			Annual interest rate		12.0%	
8			Number of monthly payments		48	
9						
10						
11						
12			Monthly payment will be:		$2,633.38	
13						
14		Payment			Principal	Principal
15		Number	Payment	Interest	Amort.	Balance
16		0				100,000.00
17		1	2,633.38	1,000.00	1,633.38	98,366.62
18		2	2,633.38	983.67	1,649.71	96,716.91
19		3	2,633.38	967.17	1,666.21	95,050.70
20		4	2,633.38	950.51	1,682.87	93,367.83
21		5	2,633.38	933.68	1,699.70	91,668.13
22		6	2,633.38	916.68	1,716.70	89,951.43
23		7	2,633.38	899.51	1,733.87	88,217.56
24		8	2,633.38	882.18	1,751.20	86,466.36
25		9	2,633.38	864.66	1,768.72	84,697.64
26		10	2,633.38	846.98	1,786.40	82,911.24
27		11	2,633.38	829.11	1,804.27	81,106.97
28		12	2,633.38	811.07	1,822.31	79,284.66
29		13	2,633.38	792.85	1,840.53	77,444.13
30		14	2,633.38	774.44	1,858.94	75,585.19
31		15	2,633.38	755.85	1,877.53	73,707.66
32		16	2,633.38	737.08	1,896.30	71,811.36
33		17	2,633.38	718.11	1,915.27	69,896.09
34		18	2,633.38	698.96	1,934.42	67,961.67

File name: **AMORTIZE** *(continued)*

	A	B	C	D	E	F
35		19	2,633.38	679.62	1,953.76	66,007.91
36		20	2,633.38	660.08	1,973.30	64,034.61
37		21	2,633.38	640.35	1,993.03	62,041.58
38		22	2,633.38	620.42	2,012.96	60,028.62
39		23	2,633.38	600.29	2,033.09	57,995.53
40		24	2,633.38	579.96	2,053.42	55,942.11
41		25	2,633.38	559.42	2,073.96	53,868.15
42		26	2,633.38	538.68	2,094.70	51,773.45
43		27	2,633.38	517.73	2,115.65	49,657.80
44		28	2,633.38	496.58	2,136.80	47,521.00
45		29	2,633.38	475.21	2,158.17	45,362.83
46		30	2,633.38	453.63	2,179.75	43,183.08
47		31	2,633.38	431.83	2,201.55	40,981.53
48		32	2,633.38	409.82	2,223.56	38,757.97
49		33	2,633.38	387.58	2,245.80	36,512.17
50		34	2,633.38	365.12	2,268.26	34,243.91
51		35	2,633.38	342.44	2,290.94	31,952.97
52		36	2,633.38	319.53	2,313.85	29,639.12
53		37	2,633.38	296.39	2,336.99	27,302.13
54		38	2,633.38	273.02	2,360.36	24,941.77
55		39	2,633.38	249.42	2,383.96	22,557.81
56		40	2,633.38	225.58	2,407.80	20,150.01
57		41	2,633.38	201.50	2,431.88	17,718.13
58		42	2,633.38	177.18	2,456.20	15,261.93
59		43	2,633.38	152.62	2,480.76	12,781.17
60		44	2,633.38	127.81	2,505.57	10,275.60
61		45	2,633.38	102.76	2,530.62	7,744.98
62		46	2,633.38	77.45	2,555.93	5,189.05
63		47	2,633.38	51.89	2,581.49	2,607.56
64		48	2,633.38	26.08	2,607.30	0.26
65						
66						

FILE NAME: BUDGET

This model demonstrates:

1.   Spreadsheet ability to organize and summarize routine financial data.

2.   Use of =SUM function.

How to use this model:

1.   Enter month in cell G6. Enter monthly budget allocations in the ranges B11 to J11.

2.   Record payments during the month under appropriate date and budget category.

3.   The totals of payment columns and the over- and under-budget amounts are automatically computed. If the payments are entered on a daily basis, the over- or under-budget amounts tell the user how much is left to spend in each budget category during that month.

4.   This model could be set up with headings and formulas as a file called BUD-GET. Each month this "blank" model would be retrieved and used. It could be saved each month using the month as the new file name.

5.   The Tools Options View could be used, then deselect the Zero values option to suppress zeros in the total column.

6.   This generally could be printed out with "Fit to 1 page" option and Landscape mode to get all columns on a single page (Page Setup).

7.   The BUDGET section of the model could be expanded to include the over- and under-budget amounts from one month as an adjustment to budget allocations for the next month. All twelve months could also be put in one spreadsheet file by creating multiple worksheets within a single workbook (see Lesson 4 for details).

The basic design features of this model include:

1.   Number formats utilized—Number (0 decimals)

2.   The single and double underlines were created with the Border button.

3.   Column widths—Column A: 7
                   —Columns B through K: 9

4.   Unprotected cells—G6, B11 to J11, B15 to J45

5.   Format Cells Border and Format Cells Pattern used to create colored heading.

The key formulas used in this model include (cell reference to left of colon; formula to right of colon):

K11: =SUM(B11:J11)   Copy to K15:K46, K49
B46: =SUM(B15:B45)   Copy to C46:J46
B49: =B11-B46   Copy to C49:J49

	A	B	C	D	E	F	G	H	I	J	K
1	Filename: BUDGET										
2	Purpose: To accumulate, summarize, and control family finances.										
3											
4					Mike and Somaya Siminski						
5					Budget Performance Report						
6					Month of JANUARY						
7											
8						BUDGET					
9		Housing &	Food &	Trans-				Contrib.			
10		Mortgage	Sundries	portation	Clothing	Medical	Recreation	& Gifts	Savings	Misc.	Total
11		675	560	200	130	90	80	70	70	75	1,950
12											
13											
14						PAYMENTS					
15	1			15			18			8	41
16	2		57							7	64
17	3										
18	4					12					12
19	5		41								41
20	6										
21	7		25							11	36
22	8	15		16		10	12				53
23	9	83	80		65						228
24	10	55						50			105
25	11										
26	12		47							5	52
27	13										
28	14		32				9				41
29	15	156	38	14							208
30	16										
31	17		35							15	50
32	18										
33	19		45	49			5				99
34	20										
35	21						11			18	29
36	22										
37	23	30	27	15	22						94
38	24										
39	25										
40	26	75									75
41	27		52					30			82
42	28										
43	29		38	12							50
44	30	360				35			70		465
45	31		58	51	18		24			8	159
46	Total	774	575	172	105	57	79	80	70	72	1,984
47	(Over)										
48	or Under										
49	Budget	(99)	(15)	28	25	33	1	(10)		3	(34)
50											

FILE NAME: BUSPLAN

This model demonstrates:

1.   Spreadsheet ability to organize and summarize lengthy calculations quickly.

2.   Ability to perform what-if analysis without using a Data Section.

3.   Use of =SUM and =NOW functions.

How to use this model:

1.   Enter data in column D for estimated start-up costs.

2.   Enter beginning cash investment in cell D28. Fill in columns G through R with monthly cash flow projections for revenues and expenditures. Note that the beginning monthly cash balances and all monthly totals are automatically computed (rows 9, 13, 31, 32, and 37). Each month should end with a positive cash balance.

3.   The totals from the cash flow projection (column S) and from the start-up cost summary (column D) are automatically carried to column V. Cell V9, V14, and V33 need to be entered directly. Enter the amounts in column X directly (totals are automatic).

The basic design features of this model include:

1.   Number formats utilized—Currency (0 decimals)
    —Number (0 decimals)
    —Percent (1 decimal)

2.   The single and double underlines were created with the Border button.

3.   Labels were aligned using the Format Cells Alignment command.

4.   Column widths—Column A: 8
    —Columns B and C: 23
    —Columns D, E, and G through T: 9
    —Columns F and U: 27
    —Columns V and X: 11
    —Columns W and Y: 7

5.   Unprotected cells—C4, D9 to D24, D28, G10 to R12, G15 to R30, G34 to R36, V9, V14, V33, X8, X9, X13, X14, X18 to X33, X37

6.   Designed to print out on four separate pages as follows:

      Page 1: Columns A through E
      Page 2: Columns F through K
      Page 3: Columns L through S
      Page 4: Columns T through Y

The key formulas used in this model include (cell reference to left of colon; formula to right of colon):

      C5:   =NOW()
      I4:   =C4
      O4:   =C4
      W4:   =C4
      D25:   =SUM(D9:D24)
      D29:   -D25
      D30:   =D28+D29
      G9:   =D30
      G13:   =SUM(G9:G12)   Copy to H13:S13
      G31:   =SUM(G15:G30)   Copy to H31:S31
      G32:   =G13-G31   Copy to H32:S32
      G37:   =G32-G34-G35-G36   Copy to H37:S37
      H9:   =G37   Copy to I9:R9
      S9:   =G9
      S10:   =SUM(G10:R10)   Copy to S11:S12, S15:S30,
                                             S34:S36

      V8:   =S10
      V10:   =V8+V9   Copy to X10
      V12:   =D11
      V13:   =S15
      V15:   =SUM(V12:V14)   Copy to X15
      V16:   =V10-V15   Copy to X16
      V18:   =S16
      V19:   =S23
      V20:   =S21
      V21:   =S24
      V22:   =(S36+D9+D12)/5
      V23:   =S18
      V24:   =S22
      V25:   =S30
      V26:   =S19
      V27:   =S26
      V28:   =S25
      V29:   =S29
      V30:   =S20
      V31:   =S28+S17
      V32:   =S27

V34: =SUM(V18:V33)   Copy to X34
V35: =V16-V34   Copy to X35
V37: =S34
V38: =V35-V37   Copy to X38
W8:   =V8/V$10   Copy to W9:W10, W12:W16,
                             W18:W35, W37:W38

X12: -V14
Y8:   =X8/X$10   Copy to Y9, Y10, Y12:Y16,
                             Y18:Y35, Y37, Y38

	A	B	C	D
1	File name: BUSPLAN			
2	Purpose: Development of a financial business plan.			
3				
4		Name of business:	Twitch's Hitches Inc.	
5		Date:	21-Feb-03	
6				
7		Start-up Costs		
8		Real estate, furniture, fixtures, equipment:		
9		a. Purchase price (if paid in full)		$10,000
10		b. Cash down payment (if financed)		0
11		Beginning inventory		80,000
12		Decorating and remodeling		20,000
13		Deposits:		
14		a. Utilities		1,000
15		b. Rents		5,000
16		c. Other		0
17		Fees:		
18		a. Legal		3,000
19		b. Accounting		3,000
20		c. Other		0
21		Initial advertising costs		5,000
22		Prestart-up salaries		0
23		Owner's drawing		10,000
24		Other		0
25		Total start-up costs		$137,000
26				
27		Owner Investment		
28		Your investment		$150,000
29		Less start-up costs		(137,000)
30		Cash available on opening day		$13,000
31				

File name: BUSPLAN *(continued)*

	F	G	H	I	J	K	L
3								
4				Twitch's Hitches Inc.			
5				Projected Cash Flow			
6								
7		1st	2nd	3rd	4th	5th	6th
8		Month	Month	Month	Month	Month	Month
9	Beginning cash (1st Month: D30)	13,000	11,150	13,200	11,200	10,200	12,200
10	Cash and credit card sales	24,000	37,000	38,000	39,000	40,000	41,000
11	Collections on credit sales		1,000	1,000	1,000	1,000	1,000
12	Loans received	10,000	5,000				
13	Total available cash	47,000	54,150	52,200	51,200	51,200	54,200
14							
15	Purchase of inventory	15,000	20,000	20,000	20,000	20,000	25,000
16	Employee wages-gross	4,000	4,000	4,000	4,000	4,000	4,000
17	Payroll taxes	600	600	600	600	600	600
18	Outside services						
19	Office supplies	500	500	500	500	500	500
20	Repairs and maintenance	1,000	1,000	1,000	1,000	1,000	1,000
21	Advertising	2,000	2,000	2,000	2,000	2,000	2,000
22	Car, delivery, travel						
23	Accounting, legal	1,250	1,250	1,250	1,250	1,250	1,250
24	Rent	2,500	2,500	2,500	2,500	2,500	2,500
25	Telephone	500	500	500	500	500	500
26	Utilities	1,500	1,500	1,500	1,500	1,500	1,500
27	Insurance	1,000	1,000	1,000	1,000	1,000	1,000
28	Real estate taxes						
29	Interest		100	150	150	150	150
30	Other expenses						
31	Total expenses	29,850	34,950	35,000	35,000	35,000	40,000
32	Cash total after expenses	17,150	19,200	17,200	16,200	16,200	14,200
33							
34	Less: Owner withdrawals	4,000	4,000	4,000	4,000	4,000	4,000
35	Loan repayments						
36	Capital expenditures	2,000	2,000	2,000	2,000		
37	Ending cash balance	11,150	13,200	11,200	10,200	12,200	10,200
38							

File name: BUSPLAN *(continued)*

	M	N	O	P	Q	R	S
3							
4			Twitch's Hitches Inc.				
5			Projected Cash Flow				
6							
7	7th	8th	9th	10th	11th	12th	Year
8	Month	Month	Month	Month	Month	Month	Summary
9	10,200	14,200	14,150	13,100	13,070	14,060	13,000
10	42,000	43,000	44,000	45,000	46,000	47,000	486,000
11	1,000	1,000	1,000	1,000	1,000	1,000	11,000
12	5,000						20,000
13	58,200	58,200	59,150	59,100	60,070	62,060	530,000
14							
15	25,000	25,000	25,000	25,000	25,000	30,000	275,000
16	4,000	4,000	4,000	4,000	4,000	4,000	48,000
17	600	600	600	600	600	600	7,200
18							0
19	500	500	500	500	500	500	6,000
20	1,000	1,000	1,000	1,000	1,000	1,000	12,000
21	2,000	2,000	2,000	2,000	2,000	2,000	24,000
22							0
23	1,250	1,250	1,250	1,250	1,250	1,250	15,000
24	2,500	2,500	2,500	2,500	2,500	2,500	30,000
25	500	500	500	500	500	500	6,000
26	1,500	1,500	1,500	1,500	1,500	1,500	18,000
27	1,000	1,000	1,000	1,000	1,000	1,000	12,000
28							0
29	150	200	200	180	160	140	1,730
30							0
31	40,000	40,050	40,050	40,030	40,010	44,990	454,930
32	18,200	18,150	19,100	19,070	20,060	17,070	75,070
33							
34	4,000	4,000	4,000	4,000	4,000	4,000	48,000
35			2,000	2,000	2,000	2,000	8,000
36							8,000
37	14,200	14,150	13,100	13,070	14,060	11,070	11,070
38							

File name: BUSPLAN *(continued)*

	U	V	W	X	Y
3					
4			Twitch's Hitches Inc.		
5			Two Year Projection of Revenues and Expenses		
6					
7		First Year		Second Year	
8	Cash & credit card sales	$486,000	97.6%	$800,000	97.6%
9	Other credit sales	12,000	2.4%	20,000	2.4%
10	Total sales	$498,000	100.0%	$820,000	100.0%
11	Cost of goods sold:				
12	Beginning inventory	80,000	16.1%	125,000	15.2%
13	Purchases	275,000	55.2%	420,000	51.2%
14	Less ending inventory	(125,000)	-25.1%	(175,000)	-21.3%
15	Total cost of goods sold	230,000	46.2%	370,000	45.1%
16	Gross profit	268,000	53.8%	450,000	54.9%
17	Expenses:				
18	Employee wages	48,000	9.6%	80,000	9.8%
19	Accounting and legal	15,000	3.0%	8,000	1.0%
20	Advertising	24,000	4.8%	50,000	6.1%
21	Rent	30,000	6.0%	30,000	3.7%
22	Depreciation	7,600	1.5%	8,000	1.0%
23	Outside services	0	0.0%	3,000	0.4%
24	Car, delivery, travel	0	0.0%	0	0.0%
25	Miscellaneous	0	0.0%	0	0.0%
26	Supplies	6,000	1.2%	9,000	1.1%
27	Electricity	18,000	3.6%	20,000	2.4%
28	Telephone	6,000	1.2%	8,000	1.0%
29	Interest	1,730	0.3%	2,500	0.3%
30	Repairs	12,000	2.4%	10,000	1.2%
31	Taxes	7,200	1.4%	15,000	1.8%
32	Insurance	12,000	2.4%	12,000	1.5%
33	Bad debts	0	0.0%	0	0.0%
34	Total expenses	187,530	37.7%	255,500	31.2%
35	Net income	80,470	16.2%	194,500	23.7%
36					
37	Less withdrawals	48,000	9.6%	80,000	9.8%
38	Net income reinvested in business	$32,470	6.5%	$114,500	14.0%
39					

FILE NAME: CHECKREG

This model demonstrates:

1.   Use of spreadsheet as a columnar journal commonly found in accounting.

2.   Use of =IF, =ROUND, and =SUM functions.

How to use this model:

1.   Set up headings and formulas on a "blank" model. Leave plenty of room for quantity of checks written each month. Save the file as CHECKREG.

2.   Each month, open in the blank model, enter the month in cell I4, and enter appropriate information in columns A through D for each check written. Then enter the amount of the check in columns E through L under the proper account category. Extra rows for more checks may be inserted if necessary.

3.   When all checks are entered, make sure the crosscheck balances. Save the file under the name of the month.

4.   Print the entire spreadsheet in the Landscape mode as a permanent record.

5.   The model could be expanded to use the =IF function to allocate check amounts to the proper account category. This could be accomplished by inserting a new column E and labeling the column "Account Number." The user would then enter the account number when typing in the other check data. Columns F through M (old columns E through L) could then be programmed with =IF statements that would enter the amount of the check in a column when the =IF statement was true; otherwise, it would enter zero. For example, assume that account numbers are entered in column E and that Cleaning supplies (moved to column G) is Account Number 7. The formula found in cell G13 would be =IF(E13=7,D13,0). Zeros could be suppressed by selecting Tools Options View and then deselecting the Zero values checkbox.

The basic design features of this model include:

1.   Number formats utilized—Number (2 decimals)

2.   The single and double underlines were created with the Borders button.

3.   Labels were aligned using the Format Cells Alignment command.

4. Column widths—Column A: 5
                    —Column B: 6
                    —Column C: 24
                    —Columns D through L: 9

5. Unprotected cells—I4, A9 to L21

6. =ROUND is needed in cell D25 to counteract very small precision errors that
    may result from summing a range of numbers.

The key formulas used in this model include (cell reference to left of colon; formula to right of colon):

D22: =SUM(D9:D21)   Copy to E22:L22
                                                         (then clear cell K22)
D25: =IF(ROUND(D22-SUM(E22:L22),0)=0,"Yes","No")

	A	B	C	D	E	F	G	H	I	J	K	L
1	File name: CHECKREG											
2	Purpose: To record checks written and to allocate checks to the correct account											
3												
4		Shoals Commercial Cleaners							Month: APRIL			
5		Check Register										
6									Account Charged			
7					Office	Cleaning	Truck		Acctg.	Licenses	Other	
8	Date	Check#	Payee	Amount	Supplies	Supplies	Expenses	Insur.	Expenses	& Fees	Account	Amount
9	3	428	Felpausch Food Store	48.22	48.22							
10	4	429	Super X Gas	17.00			17.00					
11	10	430	Fitts Accounting	55.00					55.00			
12	11	431	Jon Hall Insurance	22.50				22.50				
13	15	432	A to Z Sweeper Co.	338.00							Equip.	338.00
14	18	433	Felpausch Food Store	74.18	43.10	31.08						
15	22	434	Felpausch Food Store	18.21		18.21						
16	25	435	Super X Gas	19.00			19.00					
17	30	436	Wilking Office Supply	4.22	4.22							
18	30	-	River Forks Bank & Trust	5.00							Srv. Chrg.	5.00
19												
20												
21												
22				601.33	47.32	97.51	36.00	22.50	55.00	0.00		343.00
23												
24												
25				Yes	<== Crosscheck balance							
26												

FILE NAME: CHURCH

This model demonstrates:

1.   Use of spreadsheet to generate monthly financial reports quickly.

2.   Use of =IF and =SUM functions.

3.   Use of the Edit Paste Special command.

4.   Use of a scratch pad where data and information needed for the calculation of the answer can be placed. A scratch pad is generally kept out of sight or at the bottom of the model so that it does not confuse the model user.

5.   Use of page breaks.

How to use this model:

1.   In January, set all values in column C to zero, enter the new budget in column G, and set all values in column I to zero. Enter the month number as 1 in cell A5. Enter January 31 as the date in cell D6. Save the file as CHURCH.

2.   CHURCH will compute Budget to Date (column D) based on month number entered in cell A5. Examine the formula for cell D10 shown in the key formulas section below. In January, the Budget to Date column (column D) will show 1/12 of the total yearly budget (column G); in February, it will show 2/12 of the total; in March, 3/12; and so forth.

      There are some exceptions in column D to this general rule. For example, examine the formulas in cells D11 and D12. Post-paid gifts are late contributions for the previous year. They are usually received in January, and thus that revenue should not be apportioned out over 12 months. A regional annual conference is sponsored by this church in May. Funds are received at that time from the national church organization. Hence, this revenue is budgeted at zero ($0) until May (Month 5).

3.   To use CHURCH, follow these steps:

      a.   Open the file CHURCH which has been saved with the previous month's data (except in January).
      b.   Enter the current month number in cell A5 and enter the current month-end date in cell D6.
      c.   Edit Copy the range C10 to C88. Then click cell I10 and select Edit Paste Special. For Paste, click the Values option. For Operation, click the Add option. Then click OK. This takes the current results from column C and adds them to the Year-to-Date values in column I. Column I now contains year-to-date values for the beginning of the current month.

Finally, delete all of last month's values in column C so that you can start the new month fresh. DO NOT DELETE THE FORMULAS IN COLUMN C, JUST THE VALUES.

d. Actual data for the current month is entered in column C.

e. Review the results. Save the updated model as CHURCH. (You may wish to save each month as a separate file.)

f. The File Print command will print the financial report on two pages.

4. To test the model, do not begin with Month 10 as shown in the example. Begin with Months 1 and 2 and observe the results to see that the model is functioning correctly.

5. If the presence of rounding errors bothers you (for example, values in the range D23:D37 do not add to the value shown in cell D38—off by a penny), all formulas in the Budget-to-Date column should include the =ROUND function. For example, the formula in cell D10 would be =ROUND(A$5/12*G10,2).

The basic design features of this model include:

1. Number formats utilized—Number (2 decimals)
   —Number (0 decimals) (cell A5)

2. The single and double underlines were created with the Borders button.

3. Labels were aligned using the Format Cells Alignment command.

4. Column widths—Columns A through I: 10

5. Unprotected cells—A5, D6, C10 to C19, C23 to C37, C41 to C51, C56 to C62, C66 to C68, C72 to C85

6. Insert Page Break command used in row 53.

The key formulas used in this model include (cell reference to left of colon; formula to right of colon):

D10: (A$5/12)*G10	Copy to D13:D15, D18, D19, D23:D37, D41:D51, D56:D62, D66:D68, D72:D85
E10: =C10+I10	Copy to E11:E19, E23:E37, E41:E51, E56:E62, E66:E68, E72:E85
F10: =E10-D10	Copy to F11:F19, F23:F37, F41:F51, F56:F62, F66:F68, F72:F85

D11: =G11
D12: =IF(A5>4,G12,0)
D16: =IF(A5>2,G16,0)
D17: =IF(A5=12,G17,0)

C20: =SUM(C10:C19)	Copy to D20:G20
C38: =SUM(C23:C37)	Copy to D38:G38
C52: =SUM(C41:C51)	Copy to D52:G52
C63: =SUM(C56:C62)	Copy to D63:G63
C69: =SUM(C66:C68)	Copy to D69:G69
C86: =SUM(C72:C85)	Copy to D86:G86
C88: =C38+C52+C63+C69+C86	Copy to D88:G88
G91: =C20	
G92: =C88	
D93: =D6	
G93: =G91-G92	
G96: =E20	
G97: =E88	
G98: =G96-G97	

	A	B	C	D	E	F	G	H	I
1	File name: CHURCH								
2	Purpose: To maintain the financial data for a non-profit organization.								
3									
4	Month #			Fourth Avenue Church					Scratch
5	10			Operating Statement					Pad
6				As of October 31, 2005					//////////
7						Over			Prior Month
8			Actual	Budget	Actual	(Under)	Yearly		Actual
9	Income		for Month	to Date	to Date	Budget	Budget		to Date
10	Giving estimates		8,942.21	78,333.33	82,643.45	4,310.12	94,000.00		73701.24
11	Post paid gifts			1,260.00	1,432.50	172.50	1,260.00		1432.50
12	Annual conference			1,000.00	1,000.00	0.00	1,000.00		1000.00
13	Non-estimated receip		22.00	4,583.33	5,446.10	862.77	5,500.00		5424.10
14	Loose offerings		233.45	2,000.00	2,260.42	260.42	2,400.00		2026.97
15	Rentals		366.00	4,166.67	5,638.00	1,471.33	5,000.00		5272.00
16	Lenten offering			1,200.00	1,243.25	43.25	1,200.00		1243.25
17	Christmas offering			0.00	0.00	0.00	1,400.00		0.00
18	Budget booster		26.00	2,833.33	2,329.00	(504.33)	3,400.00		2303.00
19	Other income			1,069.17	577.09	(492.08)	1,283.00		577.09
20	Total		9,589.66	96,445.83	102,569.81	6,123.98	116,443.00		92980.15
21									
22	Salaries								
23	Pastor/salary		1,726.67	17,266.67	17,266.70	0.03	20,720.00		15540.03
24	Pastor/insurance		124.80	1,000.00	1,248.00	248.00	1,200.00		1123.20
25	Pastor/travel		200.00	2,083.33	2,291.00	207.67	2,500.00		2091.00
26	Assoc. pastor/salary		710.00	2,916.67	3,854.00	937.33	3,500.00		3144.00
27	Assoc. pastor/travel			1,666.67	1,086.75	(579.92)	2,000.00		1086.75
28	Youth worker/salary		150.00	916.67	485.00	(431.67)	1,100.00		335.00
29	Choir director/salary		366.67	3,666.67	3,666.70	0.03	4,400.00		3300.03
30	Summer organist salary			125.00	30.00	(95.00)	150.00		30.00
31	Secretary/salary		958.33	9,583.33	9,583.30	(0.03)	11,500.00		8624.97
32	Office help			350.00	262.98	(87.02)	420.00		262.98
33	Custodian/salary		400.00	4,000.00	4,000.00	0.00	4,800.00		3600.00
34	Custodial assistance			416.67	90.05	(326.62)	500.00		90.05
35	Pulpit substitutes			62.50	0.00	(62.50)	75.00		0.00
36	Pastors' conference			208.33	250.00	41.67	250.00		250.00
37	Social security tax		125.00	1,250.00	1,250.00	0.00	1,500.00		1125.00
38	Total		4,761.47	45,512.50	45,364.48	(148.02)	54,615.00		40603.01
39									
40	Program Budget								
41	Christian ed. mat'l.		38.80	750.00	1,012.67	262.67	900.00		973.87
42	Camp scholarships			333.33	400.00	66.67	400.00		400.00
43	Youth activities/jr.		61.00	83.33	94.57	11.24	100.00		33.57
44	Youth activities/sr.		8.95	83.33	64.43	(18.90)	100.00		55.48
45	Summer program			83.33	76.00	(7.33)	100.00		76.00
46	Membership & evan.		12.00	125.00	243.73	118.73	150.00		231.73
47	Missions		41.80	166.67	97.26	(69.41)	200.00		55.46
48	Publicity & p.r.		97.50	333.33	471.62	138.29	400.00		374.12
49	Special programs			125.00	196.94	71.94	150.00		196.94
50	Choir music			291.67	388.81	97.14	350.00		388.81
51	Miscellaneous			166.67	126.66	(40.01)	200.00		126.66
52	Total		260.05	2,541.67	3,172.69	631.02	3,050.00		2912.64
53									

File name: CHURCH *(continued)*

	A	B	C	D	E	F	G	H	I
54			Actual	Budget	Actual	(Under)	Yearly		Actual
55	Conference		for Month	to Date	to Date	Budget	Budget		to Date
56	World service		233.00	8,877.50	9,768.00	890.50	10,653.00		9535.00
57	Adm./salary & pens.			12,872.50	14,383.49	1,510.99	15,447.00		14383.49
58	Minis. ed. 2% fund		122.00	1,215.83	1,342.00	126.17	1,459.00		1220.00
59	Misc. askings			760.00	836.00	76.00	912.00		836.00
60	Black college fund			477.50	528.00	50.50	573.00		528.00
61	Mission priority fd.			340.83	374.00	33.17	409.00		374.00
62	Our mission concern			0.00	0.00	0.00			0.00
63	Total		355.00	24,544.17	27,231.49	2,687.32	29,453.00		26876.49
64									
65	Office								
66	Office supplies			1,666.67	1,629.16	(37.51)	2,000.00		1629.16
67	Postage		44.00	833.33	1,004.12	170.79	1,000.00		960.12
68	Stewardship cultiv.			416.67	356.16	(60.51)	500.00		356.16
69	Total		44.00	2,916.67	2,989.44	72.77	3,500.00		2945.44
70									
71	Building Upkeep								
72	Chapel rent		275.00	2,062.50	1,925.00	(137.50)	2,475.00		1650.00
73	Insurance			2,916.67	2,848.78	(67.89)	3,500.00		2848.78
74	Heat		428.71	7,500.00	7,877.00	377.00	9,000.00		7448.29
75	Electricity		134.88	1,000.00	1,118.28	118.28	1,200.00		983.40
76	Church kit. util.		300.00	833.33	1,113.86	280.53	1,000.00		813.86
77	Telephone		143.85	1,416.67	1,563.67	147.00	1,700.00		1419.82
78	Office equipment			333.33	587.01	253.68	400.00		587.01
79	Parsonage/util.		101.56	1,333.33	1,376.25	42.92	1,600.00		1274.69
80	Parsonage/repairs		27.00	208.33	313.82	105.49	250.00		286.82
81	Assoc. pastor/util.		37.71	583.33	320.00	(263.33)	700.00		282.29
82	Custodial supplies		38.02	1,458.33	1,535.39	77.06	1,750.00		1497.37
83	Organ & piano			125.00	75.00	(50.00)	150.00		75.00
84	Contingency fund		100.00	1,000.00	1,000.00	0.00	1,200.00		900.00
85	Loan repayment		83.33	833.33	833.33	(0.00)	1,000.00		750.00
86	Total		1,670.06	21,604.17	22,487.39	883.22	25,925.00		20817.33
87									
88	Combined Total Expense		7,090.58	97,119.17	101,245.49	4,126.32	116,543.00		94154.91
89									
90									
91	Operating revenue for month						9,589.66		
92	Operating expense for month						7,090.58		
93	Net for month ended			October 31, 2005			2,499.08		
94									
95									
96	Operating revenue for year to date						102,569.81		
97	Operating expense for year to date						101,245.49		
98	Net for year to date						1,324.32		
99									
100									

FILE NAME: CLASS

This model demonstrates:

1.   Use of =MAX, =MIN, =AVERAGE, =COUNT, and =VLOOKUP functions.

2.   Use of a model for record keeping and summarization.

3.   Use of Data Sort command.

How to use this model:

1.   At the beginning of the semester, set up the model with student names and numbers. Also set up the headings and all formulas.

2.   Fill in test scores as the semester progresses.

3.   Use the =VLOOKUP function to assign final grades based on points accumulated.

4.   Print the entire spreadsheet for your personal records. Print only columns C through H if you wish to publicly post the test results without disclosing student names.

5.   Since this is set up in a database format, Data commands may be used for analysis. For example, Data Sort may be used to sort the class list by final grades using the following steps: (1) select the range A10 to H25, (2) select the Data Sort command, (3) select column H to sort by, (4) select Descending, (5) click OK, and (6) click the Undo button if you've messed it up!

The basic design features of this model include:

1.   Number formats utilized—Number (0 decimals)
                              —Number (1 decimal)
                              —Percent (0 decimals)

2.   The single underlines were created with the Borders button.

3.   Labels were aligned using the Format Cells Alignment command.

4.   Column widths—Columns A and B: 9
                     —Column C: 13
                     —Columns D through H: 7

5.   Unprotected cells—D10 to F25

The key formulas used in this model include (cell reference to left of colon; formula to right of colon):

G10: =SUM(D10:F10)	Copy to G11:G25
H10: =VLOOKUP(G10,B$36:C$44,2)	Copy to H11:H25
D27: =MIN(D10:D25)	Copy to E27:H27
D28: =MAX(D10:D25)	Copy to E28:H28
D29: =AVERAGE(D10:D25)	Copy to E29:H29
D30: =COUNT(D10:D25)	Copy to E30:H30

	A	B	C	D	E	F	G	H
1	File name: CLASS							
2	Purpose: To maintain class records.							
3								
4		Class:	Advanced Excel					
5		Section:	2					
6		Term:	Fall 2005					
7		Professor:	G. Smith					
8								
9	STUDENT NAME		STUDENT #	TEST 1	TEST 2	TEST 3	TOTAL	GRADE
10	Ahmad Jayger		366-50-7989	78	58	76	212	2.0
11	Baker Holly		372-43-6400	94	92	96	282	4.0
12	Clavenna Carl		472-54-6681	56		72	128	0.0
13	Eckoff Janet		051-33-2984	96	100	98	294	4.0
14	Graham Faith		266-88-5491	58	66	68	192	1.0
15	Heidt Mary		377-54-6120	66	70	94	230	2.5
16	Jessen Julie		629-46-3309	90	76	94	260	3.5
17	Kingsmore Kathy		481-23-8172	88	92	82	262	3.5
18	Kroeger Annie		272-44-7328	92	100	98	290	4.0
19	Martenson John		482-44-2296	98	72	82	252	3.0
20	Maurice Michael		288-42-3381	94	100	80	274	4.0
21	Otten Carol		122-24-4837	86	100	88	274	4.0
22	Piper James		367-46-2457	86	100	86	272	4.0
23	Stephenson Lori		332-87-5674	82	74	82	238	2.5
24	Swallow Mary Ellen		585-82-7326	76	86	88	250	3.0
25	Yearego Anthony		723-66-1845	62	82	78	222	2.0
26								
27			Low score	56	58	68	128	0.0
28			High score	98	100	98	294	4.0
29			Average score	81.4	84.5	85.1	245.8	2.9
30			Count	16	15	16	16	16
31								
32								
33								
34			Grade Lookup Table:					
35		Scale	Points		Grade			
36		0%	0		0.0			
37		60%	180		1.0			
38		65%	195		1.5			
39		70%	210		2.0			
40		75%	225		2.5			
41		80%	240		3.0			
42		85%	255		3.5			
43		90%	270		4.0			
44		100%	300					
45								
46								

FILE NAME: COSTJOB

This model demonstrates:

1.   Automatic tabulation of costs for a job.

2.   Use of =ROUND.

How to use this model:

1.   Enter the date in cell G4 and the job number in cell G5.

2.   Fill in columns B, C, E, and F for direct materials and direct labor.

The basic design features of this model include:

1.   Number formats utilized—Number (2 decimals)
                                          —Number (0 decimals)
                                          —Percent (0 decimals)

2.   The single and double underlines were created with the Borders button.

3.   Labels were aligned using the Format Cells Alignment command and the Merge and Center button.

4.   Column widths—Columns A and G: 11
                            —Columns B through F: 9

5.   Unprotected cells—G4, G5, B9 to C11, E9 to F11, B16 to C17, E16 to F17

6.   The font used for this model is Comic Sans MS.

The key formulas used in this model include (cell reference to left of colon; formula to right of colon):

G9:   =E9*F9   Copy to G10:G11 and G16:G17
G12: =G9+G10+G11
G18: =G16+G17
D22: =E16
G22: =D22*F22
E23: =G17
G23: =ROUND(E23*F23,2)
G24: =G33+G34
G27: =G12+G18+G24

	A	B	C	D	E	F	G
1	File name: COSTJOB						
2	Purpose: Job order cost sheet for a manufacturing organization.						
3							
4		**JCD Fabricating Company**				Date	14-May-04
5		Job Cost Sheet				Job No.	9013
6							
7	Direct Materials						
8		Dept. #	Req. #		Quantity	Cost/Unit	Total
9		1	B768		780	8.29	6,466.20
10		2	B770		95	22.07	2,096.65
11							0.00
12					Total direct materials		8,562.85
13							
14	Direct Labor						
15		Dept. #	Ticket #		Hours	Rate	Total
16		1	1169-1189		178	7.25	1,290.50
17		2	2131-2134		44	8.75	385.00
18					Total direct labor		1,675.50
19							
20	Applied Factory Overhead						
21		Dept. #	Basis	Hours	Cost	Rate	Total
22		1	DL hours	178	XXXXX	4.00	712.00
23		2	DL cost	XXXXX	385.00	175%	673.75
24					Total applied overhead		1,385.75
25							
26							
27					Total factory cost		11,624.10
28							
29							

FILE NAME: FINSTMTS

This model demonstrates:

1.   Presentation of financial statements with charts.

2.   Use of =SUM function.

How to use this model:

1.   Enter financial data in cells C10 to D12, C15 to D18, B26 to H27, G29 to H29, and G31 to H31.

2.   Use the charts to help interpret the financial statements.

The basic design features of this model include:

1.   Number formats utilized—Currency (0 decimals)
                             —Number (0 decimals)

2.   The single and double underlines were created with the Borders button.

3.   Labels were aligned using the Format Cells Alignment command and the Merge and Center button.

4.   Column widths—Column A: 1
                   —Column B: 18.5
                   —Columns C, D, G, and H: 7.22
                   —Column E: 1
                   —Column F: 18

5.   Unprotected cells—C10 to D12, C15 to D18, G26 to H27, G29 to H29, G31 to H31

6.   Font—Arial MT (all text in model); Courier (all values in model)

The key formulas used in this model include (cell reference to left of colon; formula to right of colon):

C13: =SUM(C10:C12)	Copy to D13
C19: =SUM(C15:C18)	Copy to D19
G28: +G26-G27	Copy to H28
G30: +G28-G29	Copy to H30
G32: +G30-G31	Copy to H32

File name: FINSTMTS

Purpose: Presentation of financial statements with charts

Jace Toys Inc.
Financial Statements

BALANCE SHEET	2005	2004
Assets	(in 000s)	(in 000s)
Current assets	$1,404	$1,338
Plant and equipment	1,941	1,702
Long term investments	136	133
Total assets	$3,481	$3,173
Equities		
Current liabilities	$1,027	$1,099
Long term liabilities	408	369
Common stock	384	345
Retained earnings	1,662	1,360
Total liabilities & equity	$3,481	$3,173

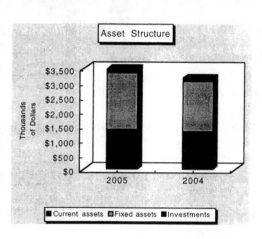

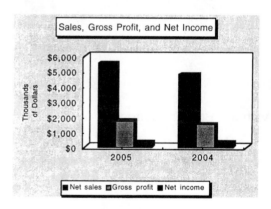

INCOME STATEMENT	2005	2004
	(in 000s)	(in 000s)
Net sales	$5,510	$4,787
Less: cost of sales	3,820	3,309
Gross profit	$1,690	$1,478
Less: expenses	1,165	964
Income before taxes	$525	$514
Provision for taxes	197	192
Net income	$328	$322

FILE NAME: INVOICE

This model demonstrates:

1.   A common business application.

2.   Use of Style Worksheet Defaults Display zeros as command.

3.   Use of =NOW and =ROUND functions.

How to use this model:

1.   Enter the invoice number in cell D4. The date is automatic.

2.   Enter the description, quantity, and unit price in columns A, B, and C, respec-
     tively. Enter the payment received in cells D21 and D22.

3.   Enter the customer information in the range A18 to A22.

4.   A print macro could be added to this worksheet to print out two copies of the
     invoice.

The basic design features of this model include:

1.   Number formats utilized—Number (2 decimals)
                             —General (0 decimals)
                             —Custom Date (mm/dd/yy)

2.   The single and double underlines were created with the Borders button.

3.   Labels were aligned using the Format Cells Alignment command and the
     Merge and Center button.

4.   Column widths—Column A: 41
                   —Columns B and D: 9
                   —Column C: 11

5.   Unprotected cells—D4, A8 to A15, B8 to B15, C8 to C15, A18 to A22, D20
                       to D22

6.   Zeros suppressed in column D by deselecting the Tools Options View Zero
     values option button.

7.   The company and address are in bold type. The headings are in italic.

The key formulas used in this model include (cell reference to left of colon; formula to right of colon):

D5:	=NOW()
D8:	+B8*C8 Copy to D9:D15
D16:	=SUM(D8:D15)
D17:	=ROUND(D16*.05,2)
D18:	+D16+17
D23:	+D18-D20-D21

	A	B	C	D
1	File name: INVOICE			
2	Purpose: Sales invoice for a retail organization.			
3				
4	**MARDI GRAS SUPPLIES INC.**		*Invoice No.*	35523
5	**Lafayette LA**		*Date*	02/21/03
6			*Unit*	
7	*Description*	*Quantity*	*Price*	*Amount*
8	Party Mask	1	23.95	23.95
9	Bead Necklaces - package of 4	5	12.88	64.40
10				
11				
12				
13				
14				
15				
16			Subtotal	88.35
17	*Customer Name*		Sales Tax	4.42
18	Andrea Stanaway		Total Due	92.77
19	119 Holiday Drive			
20	Livonia MI			
21			*Cash*	
22			*Credit Card*	92.77
23	THANK YOU FOR YOUR BUSINESS!			
24				

FILE NAME: PROPERTY

This model demonstrates:

1.   A Data Section where changeable data are entered. A Data Section is an effective way of grouping all changeable data in one place.

2.   An extensive Data Section and an extensive analysis.

3.   Example of investment analysis.

4.   Loan amortization schedule.

5.   Use of =IF, =SUM, =PMT, and =IRR functions.

6.   Use of a scratch pad where data and information needed for the calculation of the answer can be placed. A scratch pad is generally kept out of sight or at the bottom of the model so that it does not confuse the model user.

How to use this model:

1.   Enter the property name in cell F6 and fill in the rest of the Data Section. Note that in cell I10, residential rental property is treated differently (faster depreciation) than nonresidential property.

2.   The Investment Analysis section of the model first computes the monthly payment required to buy this property (using =PMT).

3.   Next, cash flow from the property is computed including the monthly mortgage payments as an expenditure.

4.   The income tax effect on the investor is then analyzed. In many cases, the write-off allowed for depreciation causes the investment to show a loss for tax purposes. Under certain circumstances, tax losses can be deducted from other income earned by an investor, and this saves the investor taxes.

5.   Finally, analyze the investment return from three different perspectives:

      a.   Return measured in dollars (rows 56-60).
      b.   Return sources as percentages (rows 64-68).
      c.   Internal rate of return (row 72).

The basic design features of this model include:

1.   Number formats utilized—Custom (0 decimals)
                                —Percent (1 decimal)
                                —Percent (0 decimals)

2. The single and double underlines were created with the Borders button.

3. Labels were aligned using the Format Cells Alignment command.

4. Column widths—Column A: 10
    —Columns B through K: 7

5. Unprotected cells—D9 to D12, D15 to D21, I9 to I10, I15 to I21

The key formulas used in this model include (cell reference to left of colon; formula to right of colon):

G26: =PMT(D11/12,D12*12,-(D9-D10))
B30: =D15
C30: =B30*(1+$I15)   Copy to D30:K30
B32: =D16   Copy to B33:B37
C32: =B32*(1+$I16)   Copy to D32:K32
C33: =B33*(1+$I17)   Copy to D33:K33
C34: =B34*(1+$I18)   Copy to D34:K34
C35: =B35*(1+$I19)   Copy to D35:K35
C36: =B36*(1+$I20)   Copy to D36:K36
C37: =B37*(1+$I21)   Copy to D37:K37
B38: =$G26*12   Copy to C38:K38
B40: =SUM(B32:B38)   Copy to C40:K40
B42: =B30-B40   Copy to C42:K42
B46: =B42   Copy to C46:K46
B47: =SUM(F99:F110)
C47: =SUM(F111:F122)
D47: =SUM(F123:F134)
E47: =SUM(F135:F146)
F47: =SUM(F147:F158)
G47: =SUM(F159:F170)
H47: =SUM(F171:F182)
I47: =SUM(F183:F194)
J47: =SUM(F195:F206)
K47: =SUM(F207:F218)
B48: =IF(($I10=1),-$D81,-$D80)   Copy to C48:K48
B50: =SUM(B46:B48)   Copy to C50:K50
B52: -B50*$I9   Copy to C52:K52
B56: =B42   Copy to C56:K56
B57: =B47   Copy to C57:K57
B58: =B52   Copy to C58:K58
B60: =SUM(B56:B58)   Copy to C60:K60
B64: =B56/B60   Copy to C64:K64
B65: =B57/B60   Copy to C65:K65
B66: =B58/B60   Copy to C66:K66
B68: =SUM(B64:B66)   Copy to C68:K68

B72: =IRR(A86:K86,.25)
C72: =IRR(.25,B87:K87)
D72: =IRR(.25,C88:K88)
E72: =IRR(.25,D89:K89)
F72: =IRR(.25,E90:K90)
G72: =IRR(.25,F91:K91)
H72: =IRR(.25,G92:K92)
I72:   =IRR(.25,H93:K93)
J72: =IRR(.25,I94:K94)
K72: =IRR(.25,J95:K95)
D80: =D9/39
D81: =D9/27.5
B85: =D10
C85: =B57+B85   Copy to D85:K85
A86: -D10
B86: =B60   Copy to C86:J86
K86: =K60+B85
B87: -C$85   Copy to C88, D89, E90, F91,
                                            G92, H93, I94, J95
C87: =C60   Copy to D87:J87
K87: =K60+C85
D88: =D60   Copy to E88:J88
K88: =K60+D85
E89: =E60   Copy to F89:J89
K89: =K60+E85
F90: =F60   Copy to G90:J90
K90: =K60+F85
G91: =G60   Copy to H91:J91
K91: =K60+G85
H92: =H60   Copy to I92:J92
K92: =K60+H85
I93:   =I60   Copy to J93
K93: =K60+I85
J94: =J60
K94: =K60+J85
K95: =K60+K85
B98: 0
H98: =D9-D10
B99: 1+B98   Copy to B100:B218
D99: =H98*D$11/12   Copy to D100:D218
F99: =G$26-D99   Copy to F100:F218
H99: =H98-F99   Copy to H100:H218

	A	B	C	D	E	F	G	H	I	J	K
1	File name: PROPERTY										
2	Purpose: 10-year cash flow and profitability projections for real estate investments										
3											
4				DATA SECTION							
5											
6			Property name:			HICKORY WOODS APARTMENTS					
7											
8	Property Data					Tax Data					
9	Cost			325000		Owner's tax bracket			28%		
10	Down payment			50000		Residential? (yes=1)			1		
11	Interest rate			11%							
12	Debt period in years			25							
13											
14	Operating Data: First Year					Operating Trends: Annual Growth %					
15	Rental collections			64800		Rental collections			4.2%		
16	Management fees			3240		Management fees			4.2%		
17	Other admin. costs			1200		Other admin. costs			2.0%		
18	Utilities			5900		Utilities			6.0%		
19	Maint. and repairs			9000		Maint. and repairs			3.0%		
20	Real estate taxes			10000		Real estate taxes			4.2%		
21	Insurance			1300		Insurance			3.0%		
22											
23											
24				INVESTMENT ANALYSIS							
25											
26			Monthly mortgage payment				2695				
27											
28				Cash Flow Projections							
29		Year1	Year2	Year3	Year4	Year5	Year6	Year7	Year8	Year9	Year10
30	Rents	64800	67522	70358	73313	76392	79600	82943	86427	90057	93839
31											
32	Mgt. fees	3240	3376	3518	3666	3820	3980	4147	4321	4503	4692
33	Admin.	1200	1224	1248	1273	1299	1325	1351	1378	1406	1434
34	Utilities	5900	6254	6629	7027	7449	7896	8369	8871	9404	9968
35	Maint.	9000	9270	9548	9835	10130	10433	10746	11069	11401	11743
36	Taxes	10000	10420	10858	11314	11789	12284	12800	13337	13898	14481
37	Insurance	1300	1339	1379	1421	1463	1507	1552	1599	1647	1696
38	Mortgage	32344	32344	32344	32344	32344	32344	32344	32344	32344	32344
39											
40	Total exp.	62984	64227	65524	66879	68292	69769	71310	72920	74602	76358
41											
42	Cash flow	1816	3295	4833	6434	8099	9831	11633	13507	15455	17481
43											
44											
45				Income Tax Effects							
46	Cash flow	1816	3295	4833	6434	8099	9831	11633	13507	15455	17481
47	+ Principal	2203	2457	2742	3059	3413	3808	4249	4740	5289	5901
48	- Deprec.	-11818	-11818	-11818	-11818	-11818	-11818	-11818	-11818	-11818	-11818
49											
50	Tax income	-7799	-6066	-4243	-2325	-306	1821	4064	6429	8926	11564
51											
52	Tax savings	2184	1698	1188	651	86	-510	-1138	-1800	-2499	-3238
53											
54											

File name: PROPERTY *(continued)*

	A	B	C	D	E	F	G	H	I	J	K
55					Investment Analysis						
56	Cash flow	1816	3295	4833	6434	8099	9831	11633	13507	15455	17481
57	Principal	2203	2457	2742	3059	3413	3808	4249	4740	5289	5901
58	Tax savings	2184	1698	1188	651	86	-510	-1138	-1800	-2499	-3238
59											
60	Return	6203	7451	8763	10144	11598	13130	14744	16447	18245	20144
61											
62											
63					Where does the return come from?						
64	Cash flow	29%	44%	55%	63%	70%	75%	79%	82%	85%	87%
65	Principal	36%	33%	31%	30%	29%	29%	29%	29%	29%	29%
66	Tax savings	35%	23%	14%	6%	1%	-4%	-8%	-11%	-14%	-16%
67											
68	Total	100%	100%	100%	100%	100%	100%	100%	100%	100%	100%
69											
70											
71					Internal Rate of Return						
72	IRR	21%	22%	23%	24%	24%	25%	25%	25%	25%	25%
73											
74											
75											
76											
77											
78	Scratch Pad:										
79				Depreciation Schedule							
80	Nonresidential rental			8333							
81	Residential rental			11818							
82											
83				Internal Rate of Return Table							
84											
85	Investment	50000	52203	54660	57402	60461	63874	67682	71931	76671	81960
86	-50000	6203	7451	8763	10144	11598	13130	14744	16447	18245	70144
87		-52203	7451	8763	10144	11598	13130	14744	16447	18245	72347
88			-54660	8763	10144	11598	13130	14744	16447	18245	74804
89				-57402	10144	11598	13130	14744	16447	18245	77546
90					-60461	11598	13130	14744	16447	18245	80605
91						-63874	13130	14744	16447	18245	84018
92							-67682	14744	16447	18245	87826
93								-71931	16447	18245	92075
94									-76671	18245	96815
95										-81960	102104

File name: PROPERTY *(continued)*

	A	B	C	D	E	F	G	H
96				Amortization Schedule				
97		Period		Interest		Principal		Balance
98		0						275000
99		1		2521		174		274826
100		2		2519		176		274649
101		3		2518		178		274472
102		4		2516		179		274292
103		5		2514		181		274111
104		6		2513		183		273929
105		7		2511		184		273745
106		8		2509		186		273559
107		9		2508		188		273371
108		10		2506		189		273181
109		11		2504		191		272990
110		12		2502		193		272797
111		13		2501		195		272603
112		14		2499		196		272406
113		15		2497		198		272208
114		16		2495		200		272008
115		17		2493		202		271806
116		18		2492		204		271602
117		19		2490		206		271397
118		20		2488		208		271189
119		21		2486		209		270980
120		22		2484		211		270768
121		23		2482		213		270555
122		24		2480		215		270340
123		25		2478		217		270123
124		26		2476		219		269904
125		27		2474		221		269682
126		28		2472		223		269459
127		29		2470		225		269234
128		30		2468		227		269007
129		31		2466		229		268777
130		32		2464		232		268546
131		33		2462		234		268312
132		34		2460		236		268076
133		35		2457		238		267838
134		36		2455		240		267598
135		37		2453		242		267356
136		38		2451		245		267111
137		39		2449		247		266864
138		40		2446		249		266615

File name: PROPERTY *(continued)*

	A	B	C	D	E	F	G	H
139		41		2444		251		266364
140		42		2442		254		266110
141		43		2439		256		265854
142		44		2437		258		265596
143		45		2435		261		265335
144		46		2432		263		265072
145		47		2430		265		264807
146		48		2427		268		264539
147		49		2425		270		264269
148		50		2422		273		263996
149		51		2420		275		263720
150		52		2417		278		263443
151		53		2415		280		263162
152		54		2412		283		262879
153		55		2410		286		262594
154		56		2407		288		262305
155		57		2404		291		262015
156		58		2402		294		261721
157		59		2399		296		261425
158		60		2396		299		261126
159		61		2394		302		260824
160		62		2391		304		260520
161		63		2388		307		260213
162		64		2385		310		259903
163		65		2382		313		259590
164		66		2380		316		259274
165		67		2377		319		258955
166		68		2374		322		258634
167		69		2371		325		258309
168		70		2368		327		257982
169		71		2365		330		257651
170		72		2362		334		257318
171		73		2359		337		256981
172		74		2356		340		256642
173		75		2353		343		256299
174		76		2349		346		255953
175		77		2346		349		255604
176		78		2343		352		255252
177		79		2340		356		254896
178		80		2337		359		254537

File name: PROPERTY *(continued)*

	A	B	C	D	E	F	G	H
179		81		2333		362		254175
180		82		2330		365		253810
181		83		2327		369		253441
182		84		2323		372		253069
183		85		2320		376		252694
184		86		2316		379		252315
185		87		2313		382		251932
186		88		2309		386		251546
187		89		2306		389		251157
188		90		2302		393		250764
189		91		2299		397		250367
190		92		2295		400		249967
191		93		2291		404		249563
192		94		2288		408		249155
193		95		2284		411		248744
194		96		2280		415		248329
195		97		2276		419		247910
196		98		2273		423		247487
197		99		2269		427		247060
198		100		2265		431		246630
199		101		2261		435		246195
200		102		2257		439		245757
201		103		2253		443		245314
202		104		2249		447		244867
203		105		2245		451		244417
204		106		2240		455		243962
205		107		2236		459		243503
206		108		2232		463		243040
207		109		2228		467		242572
208		110		2224		472		242100
209		111		2219		476		241624
210		112		2215		480		241144
211		113		2210		485		240659
212		114		2206		489		240170
213		115		2202		494		239676
214		116		2197		498		239178
215		117		2192		503		238675
216		118		2188		507		238168
217		119		2183		512		237655
218		120		2179		517		237139

FILE NAME: RATIO

This model demonstrates:

1. A Data Section where changeable data are entered. A Data Section is an effective way of grouping all changeable data in one place.

2. Example of ratio analysis.

How to use this model:

1. At the end of each year, enter selected financial information obtained from the company's annual report into the Data Section (Selected Financial Input).

2. Copy the formulas in the Analysis section into the column containing the financial data for a new year.

3. Comments on ratios:

    a. Year-end balances rather than average balances for accounts receivable and inventory were used in the turnover ratios.
    b. Year-end balances rather than average balances for total assets and stockholders' equity were used for the return ratios.
    c. To compute the accounts receivable turnover ratio, all sales were assumed to be on credit.

4. The landscape mode could be used to print out the model if there are more than five years of data.

5. The model could be used to compare companies in a similar industry. Instead of using consecutive years as the column heading, pick one year and enter the name of each company to be analyzed at the top of each column. Use the model to compare ratios each year among selected companies.

The basic design features of this model include:

1. Number formats utilized—Number (0 decimals)
    —Number (2 decimals)
    —Percent (2 decimals)
    —Percent (0 decimals)

2. The single and double underlines were created with the Borders button.

3. Labels were aligned using the Format Cells Alignment command.

4.   Column widths—Column A: 24
                          —Columns B through F: 9

5.   Unprotected cells—B4, B7 to F26

The key formulas used in this model include (cell reference to left of colon; formula to right of colon):

B30: =B10/B13	Copy to other columns
B31: =(B7+B8)/B13	Copy to other columns
B32: =B18/B8	Copy to other columns
B33: =B19/B9	Copy to other columns
B34: =(B24+B22)/B11	Copy to other columns
B35: =B24/B15	Copy to other columns
B36: =B14/B11	Copy to other columns
B37: =B26/B24	Copy to other columns
B38: =B21/B22	Copy to other columns
B40: =B10/B11	Copy to other columns
B41: =(B11-B10)/B11	Copy to other columns
B42: =B11/B11	Copy to other columns
B44: =B13/B16	Copy to other columns
B45: =(B14-B13)/B16	Copy to other columns
B46: =B15/B16	Copy to other columns
B47: =B16/B16	Copy to other columns
B49: =B18/B18	Copy to other columns
B50: =B20/B18	Copy to other columns
B51: =B21/B18	Copy to other columns
B52: =B24/B18	Copy to other columns

	A	B	C	D	E	F
1	File name: RATIO					
2	Purpose: To maintain an ongoing record of company financial ratios.					
3						
4		Arbor Graphics, Inc.				
5						
6	SELECTED FINANCIAL INPUT	2001	2002	2003	2004	2005
7	Cash and equivalents	120	90	168		
8	Accounts receivable	1,896	2,065	2,222		
9	Inventory	3,836	4,154	5,384		
10	Current assets	6,036	6,554	8,151		
11	Total assets	19,482	21,437	36,960		
12						
13	Current liabilities	4,678	5,164	7,969		
14	Total liabilities	13,827	14,614	29,281		
15	Stockholders' equity	5,655	6,823	7,679		
16	Total liab. & equity	19,482	21,437	36,960		
17						
18	Sales	25,883	28,183	31,742		
19	Cost of goods sold	16,088	17,010	18,739		
20	Gross profit	9,795	11,173	13,003		
21	Operating income	3,537	3,990	4,670		
22	Interest expense	772	646	670		
23	Income taxes	1,287	1,502	1,663		
24	Net income	1,478	1,842	2,337		
25						
26	Dividends	590	674	1,481		
27						
28						
29	ANALYSIS	2001	2002	2003	2004	2005
30	Current ratio	1.29	1.27	1.02		
31	Quick ratio	0.43	0.42	0.30		
32	Accts. receivable turnover	13.65	13.65	14.29		
33	Inventory turnover	4.19	4.09	3.48		
34	Return on assets	11.55%	11.61%	8.14%		
35	Return on equity	26.14%	27.00%	30.43%		
36	Debt to total assets	70.97%	68.17%	79.22%		
37	Dividend payout ratio	39.92%	36.59%	63.37%		
38	Times-interest-earned	4.58	6.18	6.97		
39	Balance sheet (%)					
40	Current assets	31%	31%	22%		
41	Long term assets	69%	69%	78%		
42	Total assets	100%	100%	100%		
43						
44	Current liabilities	24%	24%	22%		
45	Long term liabilities	47%	44%	58%		
46	Stockholders' equity	29%	32%	21%		
47	Total liab. & equity	100%	100%	100%		
48	Income Statement (%)					
49	Sales	100%	100%	100%		
50	Gross profit	38%	40%	41%		
51	Operating income	14%	14%	15%		
52	Net income	6%	7%	7%		
53						

FILE NAME: REORDER

This model demonstrates:

1.   Database for inventory control.

2.   Use of Custom date format.

How to use this model:

1.   Enter updated quantity on hand (column D) at regular intervals, and reorder when needed.

2.   Enter updated information in other columns on a timely basis as changes occur.

3.   Use the Data Sort command when you wish to reorganize the information presented. The most obvious columns for sorting would be columns A, C, and G.

The basic design features of this model include:

1.   Number formats utilized—General (0 decimals)
                                 —Custom date format dd-mmm-yy (column G)

2.   The single underlines were created with the Borders button.

3.   Labels were aligned using the Format Cells Alignment command and the Merge and Center button.

4.   Column widths—Column A: 8
                    —Column B: 15
                    —Columns C through G: 9

5.   Unprotected cells—D10 to D29

The key formulas used in this model include (cell reference to left of colon; formula to right of colon):

No formulas were used in this model.

	A	B	C	D	E	F	G
1	File name: REORDER						
2	Purpose: Inventory reorder database						
3							
4			Inventory Control Report				
5			Alligator Boat Supplies				
6			August 25, 2005				
7							
8	ITEM			QUANTITY	REORDER	ORDER	LAST
9	NUMBER	DESCRIPTION	LOCATION	ON HAND	LEVEL	QUANTITY	ORDER
10	1223	Motor Drive Assy	Factory	22	25	25	14-Jun-05
11	1326	Cleated Roller	Factory	4	2	10	22-Dec-04
12	1529	3/8 F Washer	Factory	2730	800	10000	19-Aug-05
13	1531	5/16 Flat Washer	Factory	200	200	1000	23-Sep-04
14	1554	1/4 F Washer	Factory	1550	500	5000	21-Jan-05
15	2000	Roller Assy	Crib	35	5	50	03-Jun-05
16	2400	Steel Frame	Warehouse	17	10	15	23-Oct-04
17	3010	Safety Rail	Dock	5	4	6	03-Sep-03
18	3020	Backrail	Dock	6	4	6	12-Dec-04
19	4000	Wiper Assy	Dock	2	2	10	31-Jan-05
20	4300	Sensor Assy	Factory	3	2	10	30-Jun-05
21	4308	Harness	Bin D	6	3	10	22-May-05
22	8002	Serial # Plate	Factory	175	200	2500	19-Aug-05
23	8003	Half Strap	Bin D	38	20	50	10-Sep-04
24	8004	Rubber Bumper	Dock	6	5	10	19-Sep-03
25	8010	Patent Decal	Bin D	425	200	1000	31-Jan-05
26	8011	Cleaning Decal	Bin D	330	200	1000	11-May-05
27	8012	Nylon F Washer	Factory	2800	1000	5000	18-Jan-05
28	8013	Panhead Phillips	Dock	870	500	5000	06-Mar-05
29	8022	Silicon Sealant	Bin A2	6	2	5	13-Oct-04
30							

FILE NAME: SUMMARY

This model demonstrates:

1. Multiple worksheets in a single workbook. The first sheet in the workbook is named SUMMARY. The next three sheets are named PROGRAM1, PRO-GRAM2, and PROGRAM3, respectively.

2. Formulas in a summary worksheet linked to cells in detail worksheets.

3. How to create a consolidated budget for a multi-division organization.

4. Use of =SUM function.

How to use this model:

1. Enter the expenditures in the individual budgets for each of the three Program worksheets.

2. Enter the revenues in the top section of the Summary worksheet.

3. The expenditures for the three programs appear automatically in rows 12-15 on the Summary worksheet. Any subsequent changes to the expenditures in the Program budget worksheets will be automatically reflected in the Summary worksheet.

The basic design features of this model include:

1. Number formats utilized—Currency (0 decimals)
    —Number (0 decimals)

2. The single and double underlines were created with the Borders button.

3. Labels were aligned using the Format Cells Alignment command.

4. Column widths—Column A (Summary): 19
    —Columns B through E (Summary): 11
    —Column A (Program): 32
    —Column B (Program): 8.11

5. Unprotected cells—Program1: B9 to B13, B16, B19 to B20, B24 to B25
    —Program2: B9 to B13, B16, B19, B22 to B24
    —Program3: B9 to B12, B15, B18, B21 to B23
    —Summary: E7 to E8

6. Cells B4 and B5 use the Terminal font with a point size of 12.

The key formulas used in this model include (cell reference to left of colon; formula to right of colon):

Summary:
    E9:   =SUM(E7:E8)
    B12: =Program1!B14
    B13: =Program1!B16
    B14: =Program1!B21
    B15: =Program1!B26
    B16: =SUM(B12:B15)   Copy to C16:E16
    C12: =Program2!B14
    C13: =Program2!B16
    C14: =Program2!B19
    C15: =Program2!B25
    D12: =Program3!B13
    D13: =Program3!B15
    D14: =Program3!B18
    D15: =Program3!B24
    E12: =SUM(B12:D12)   Copy to E13:E15
    E18: =E9-E16

Program1:
    B14: =SUM(B9:B13)
    B21: =SUM(B19:B20)
    B26: =SUM(B24:B25)

Program2:
    B14: =SUM(B9:B13)
    B25: =SUM(B22:B24)

Program3:
    B13: =SUM(B9:B12)
    B24: =SUM(B21:B23)

	A	B	C	D	E
1	File name: SUMMARY				
2	Purpose: To consolidate budgets in a multi-divisional organization.				
3					
4			**Feller Foundation**		
5			**Annual Budget**		
6	Revenues:				
7	Government grants				$150,000
8	Private donations				308,165
9	Total Revenues				$458,165
10					
11	Expenditures:	Program 1	Program 2	Program 3	Total
12	Salaries	$159,600	$67,850	$44,600	$272,050
13	Rents	12,415	7,500	6,800	26,715
14	Research Grants	13,700	6,500	10,000	30,200
15	Supplies	52,300	49,400	27,500	129,200
16	Total Expenditures	$238,015	$131,250	$88,900	$458,165
17					
18	Excess of revenues over expenditures				$0
19					

	A	B
1	File name: PROGRAM1	
2	Purpose: To accumulate budget data for a division	
3		
4	Program 1	
5	The Medical Clinic	
6	Annual Expenses	
7		
8	Salaries	
9	Dr. Jim Jones, MD	$55,000
10	Dr. Mary Thomas, MD	50,000
11	Mrs. Gloria Jackson	18,500
12	Mr. Joe Smith	17,000
13	Ms. Jane Q. Citizen	19,100
14	Total	$159,600
15		
16	Rent (annual)	$12,415
17		
18	Research Grants	
19	Alcoholism and Drug Abuse	$6,500
20	Curing the Common Cold	7,200
21	Total	$13,700
22		
23	Supplies	
24	Medical	$36,800
25	Administrative	15,500
26	Total	$52,300
27		
28		

	A	B
1	File name: PROGRAM2	
2	Purpose: To accumulate budget data for a division	
3		
4	Program 2	
5	Inner City Revival	
6	Annual Expenses	
7		
8	Salaries	
9	Joe Bradley	$12,700
10	Maria Cortez	11,750
11	Roland O'Neill	14,000
12	John Mattichak	17,000
13	Delores Johnstone	12,400
14	Total	$67,850
15		
16	Rent (annual)	$7,500
17		
18	Research Grant	
19	Improving the Inner City	$6,500
20		
21	Supplies	
22	City Park improvements	$25,200
23	Apartment improvements	13,700
24	Administrative	10,500
25	Total	$49,400
26		
27		

	A	B
1	File name: PROGRAM3	
2	Purpose: To accumulate budget data for a division	
3		
4	Program 3	
5	Recycle Deboise	
6	Annual Expenses	
7		
8	Salaries	
9	Clifford Crane	$10,500
10	Michael D. Angelo	10,500
11	Betty Wentworth	12,600
12	Buford Smith	11,000
13	Total	$44,600
14		
15	Rent (annual)	$6,800
16		
17	Research Grant	
18	Save Energy (Recycle)	$10,000
19		
20	Supplies	
21	Fork lift	$17,500
22	Barrels	2,500
23	Administrative	7,500
24	Total	$27,500
25		
26		

FILE NAME: TAXCOMP

This model demonstrates:

1. A Data Section where changeable data are entered. A Data Section is an effective way of grouping all changeable data in one place.

2. A simple Data Section and a simple Answer Section with a complex formula.

3. Use of =VLOOKUP function.

4. Use of a scratch pad where data and information needed for the calculation of the answer can be placed. A scratch pad is generally kept out of sight or at the bottom of the model so that it does not confuse the model user.

How to use this model:

1. Obtain (or compute) the taxpayer's taxable income and enter it in cell E6. The answer gives the taxpayer's tax bracket and total tax liability (using hypothetical rates).

2. Change the information for each different taxpayer.

3. Change the lookup table to reflect changes in the tax law.

The basic design features of this model include:

1. Number formats utilized—Currency (2 decimals)
                                        —General (0 and 1 decimals)
                                        —Percent (0 and 1 decimals)

2. The single and double underlines were created with the Borders button.

3. Labels were aligned using the Format Cells Alignment command.

4. Column widths—Columns A through D and F: 9
                              —Column E: 14

5. Unprotected cells—E6

The key formulas used in this model include (cell reference to left of colon; formula to right of colon):

    F9:   =VLOOKUP(E6,B18:E23,4)
    F10: =VLOOKUP(E6,B18:E23,3)+((E6-VLOOKUP(E6,B18:E23,2))*E9)

	A	B	C	D	E	F
1	File name: TAXCOMP					
2	Purpose: Compute tax bracket and tax liability for single individuals					
3						
4						
5			**Data Section**			
6		Enter taxable income			$75,382	
7						
8			**Answer Section**			
9		Your marginal tax bracket is			30.0%	
10		Your tax liability is			$16,929.60 *	
11						
12						
13		* Note: If your taxable income is below $100,000, you must use				
14		IRS tax tables. Because the IRS rounds off its tables, the actual				
15		tax you owe the IRS will be slightly more or slightly less than the				
16		amount computed above.				
17						
18						
19						
20						
21				Scratch Pad	(2002 rates)	
22		Taxable	Taxable	Tax on	Tax Rate	
23		Income	Base	Base	On Excess	
24		0	0	0	10%	
25		6000	6000	600	15%	
26		27950	27950	3892.5	27%	
27		67700	67700	14625	30%	
28		141250	141250	36690	35%	
29		307050	307050	94720	38.6%	
30						

Index